Avelynn is an inspiration to all who have met her…her exceptional determination, tenacity, and wacky sense of humour allow her to cope with new and serious health issues.

Michelle and Bronwyn, Nurse Consultants, Cardiology Dept.,
Royal Children's Hospital, Melbourne

Avelynn has taught me how to be a better person and parent… her determination is the most remarkable achievement and her courage exceeds all expectations. Michelle's relentless will and effort to never give up will astound you and take you far beyond what you think you are capable of. Avelynn is in the truest sense, a ray of pure sunshine.

Mum of two, Melbourne

One of the wonderful things about working for Starlight is the opportunity to meet amazing people…Avelynn and her family certainly are amazing. Thank you for the positive impact you have on the lives of others.

Jo Dann, Starlight Children's Foundation

Within the first ten weeks of her life Avelynn endured two major open heart surgeries, had six heart attacks, suffered a stroke and yet somehow survived. Avelynn is now twelve years old and lives with five incurable diseases as well as her heart problem. Of course, her feisty attitude and wicked sense of humour helps.

Yet, Michelle's book is not a "woe is me" story, it is a story that celebrates life and living to the full and how to endure and overcome adversity and the doctors' grim diagnosis.

The book talks about learning about, and coping with, the fact that Michelle's baby had something wrong with her heart. Reaching out to others such as family, and friends like HeartKids, for the support they offer, the long phone chats at all times of the day.

Unfortunately, with childhood heart disease as prevalent as it is in Australia, it is an all too common story but it is one that takes courage and perspective to live through and then share with others as Michelle is doing.

Terry Hopkins, CEO, HeartKids [illegible]

$150 bonus

To claim your free bonus, go to

www.michellewood.com.au

Discover 101 Ways
to a Healthier Body and More!

My Little Red Head

The extraordinary, true, amazing, and amusing story of how Avelynn survived heart disease

by

Michelle Wood

Woodduck
Press
Melbourne

Published by Woodduck Press, Melbourne, Australia.
To contact Woodduck Press, email: 1michellegwood@gmail.com

While the author has made every effort to provide accurate Internet addresses at the time of publication, neither the publisher nor the author assume any responsibility for errors, or for changes that occur after publication. Neither the publisher nor the author have any control over or assume any responsibility for third-party web sites or their content.

Logo, book, and cover design by David E. Brown

First edition: December, 2011

ISBN 978-0-9872415-2-8

Printed in USA

10 9 8 7 6 5 4 3 2 1

Neither the author nor the publisher are engaged in rendering professional advice or services to the individual reader. The ideas, information, and suggestions in this book are not intended as substitutes for consulting a physician or other health care provider. All matters regarding health require medical advice or supervision. Neither the author nor the publisher shall be liable for any loss or damage allegedly arising from any idea, information, or suggestion in this book.

Contents

Forward

I am a paediatric cardiac surgeon at the Royal Children's Hospital in Melbourne and as such, I have had to operate on Avelynn five times since she was born. Avelynn is an extraordinary young girl whose story impresses and humbles all of us who have been in contact with her. It is with great pleasure that I write a foreword for Michelle's book.

The relationship between a paediatric cardiac surgeon and his patient's parents and most evidently the patient's mother is very unbalanced. On the parents' side, it is emotional, it is profound and I am told leaves deep memories of what usually is a relatively short stay in the hospital, a few days, two weeks at the most for nearly all of our patients. We surgeons on the other side perform surgery in a few hours and then when the patient does well, which is fortunately the rule, we only have a few brief ward rounds to build a relationship with the family, an attachment to the child and his parents. Almost invariably, we loose all contact with people who are immensely grateful to us and our work.

Avelynn's story is different. Avelynn came to us at two months of age, with a fairly complex cardiac anomaly, although not uncommon. She should have normally faded into oblivion as many of our patients who have done well. Unfortunately, this was not the case. Evelyn's physiology was different than usually and very wrong. As soon as her surgery was completed we could tell that her pulmonary artery pressure was very high, grossly elevated and we knew that she would have to brace for a fight, a long fight; we at the Royal Children's Hospital remember every step of it. Avelynn has gone through horrendous times and she lived. She embraces life but we have not cured her.

Avelynn's story is about hope and the incredible will to live and to defy the odds stacked up against her. It is about the energy required to live with chronic illness.

It is also about the strength generated by her little being, how it transforms and inspires the lives of her family but also gives the strength and motivation for all of us involved in her care to continue fighting for each of our patients life, whatever the hours and the difficulty.

Congenital Heart defect is the most common congenital anomaly. It is the most common cause of death for children under the age of five with more than four young Australians dying each week as a result. Paediatric cardiac surgery, the surgical correction of heart defect, has made tremendous progresses in the last three decades; however, not all cardiac defects can be cured and not all surgery lead to a smooth and simple post-operative course.

Michele's book gives insight into her family's courageous struggle as they cope with the emotional medical and personal turmoil of Avelynn's fight to live. This book is unlike any other as it explores and describes the consequences of Avelynn diagnosis, treatment and then chronic illness on her family through he viewpoint of Michelle, her mum. How Michelle coped with the diagnosis of congenital heart disease, the roller coaster of the first operation and the effects that Avelynn's chronic illness had on her family. Michelle explores the stress, difficulties she and her family faced and how they adapted to these challenges. Michelle's book demonstrates how the diagnosis of congenital cardiac anomaly in one of the siblings can profoundly affect a whole family.

The book shows how important it is for us to continue researching as we do through the Heart Research Centre at the Murdoch Children's Research Institute at the Royal Children's Hospital, but also that the focus of research should be multiple: Basic research, translational research, clinical research and impact of the condition on the patient and his family.

I wish that Michelle's book will have as large an audience as possible and will change each readers' life at least a little.

And to all, best reading.

Kind regards,

A/Prof Christian Brizard

Welcome to My Book

This is the first book in a trilogy of my daughter's life. Against the odds, as Avelynn continues to prosper, ten years after she was expected to die at the age of two.

Avelynn has survived for twelve years with a congenital heart defect and five rare, incurable diseases:

- Pulmonary hypertension
- Portal hypertension
- Cirrhosis of the liver with oesophageal varicies
- Pancytopenia, a blood disorder of the spleen
- Protein-losing enteropathy, a digestive disorder

She also lives with an incurable congenital heart defect and faces additional open-heart surgeries as she grows older. Oops! I forgot to mention that she had a stroke as a baby.

Whilst Avelynn is a fighter (and amazing) I would like to acknowledge other children who have fought against the odds and have come up trumps, and sadly, those that have bravely fought, but lost their battles.

This book is testament to the triumph of the human spirit, which can endure incredible challenges yet makes you question life. Why we are here? What is our purpose? Each of us has hidden strengths that we don't suspect. These only surface as we meet extraordinary challenges, and these make us better people.

Avelynn is a gift to our family, and for her we are eternally grateful. We wouldn't change a thing. Without her, we wouldn't know how strong we are as a family, . We have maintained our senses of humour and a positive attitude to life; both are essential skills. And we are again truly grateful to Avelynn for her wacky, sometimes outrageous, sense of humour. This helps her and us get through our days.

Avelynn has helped me face the challenges of my early life, to run with my fear, to not fear what lies ahead, to live but one day at a time, and to keep my dreams alive.

Michelle Wood

Acknowledgements

Writing *My Little Red Head* has been an extraordinary experience for me, at times challenging, and other times inspiring.

As with any major project, a number of special people contributed, indirectly and directly, to making this book happen.

Firstly, to my husband, Peter, for his never-ending support during the times when it all seemed too overwhelming for me to continue.

To my beautiful, amazing, and inspiring children Ayla, Kara, and Avelynn, who have the utmost faith in me, "that mum can do anything."

To my special "mankie boy," Mungo, for especially his endless supply of love and cuddles that supported me through thick and thin.

To Dr John Demartini, for whom I am eternally grateful for sharing his insightful knowledge about life and showing me that every cloud has a silver lining.

And finally to the medical staffs at The Royal Children's Hospital in Melbourne and Princess Margaret Hospital in Perth, for believing in Avelynn, and fighting for her.

Happy first birthday—yummy cake time

Do you like my chook?
Kara and Avelynn, 2,
in Queensland

Avelynn, two years old,
in Brisbane

Chapter 1

Where Avelynn Got Her Strength

My husband Peter and I grew up in Australia and our parents are Australian born and bred. However, we lived on opposite sides of the country. Our cultures, climates, and family situations were so different, that we might as well have been born on opposite sides of the world.

You would be hard-pressed to find two people who were brought up so differently, yet through circumstances beyond our understanding met, married, and matched each other perfectly.

I was born on New Year's Eve in 1966, but no one celebrated my arrival. My grandfather had just lost a contest with a train to see who could get to a crossing faster. He didn't quite make it before the train hit his car, killing him instantly. He was from New South Wales, half-way up the east coast of Australia.

Grandfather had just bought a business up north in Queensland and hoped to move there soon with my grandmother, "Nana." He was driving there when he lost to the train. We never knew who was at fault. Nana had the sad burden of telling her son Geoff and my mum that their well-loved step dad had died. My mum, pregnant with me, went into shock and labour at the news.

After much driving around from one relative to the next, my mum eventually arrived at the Lilydale Bush Nursing Hospital, in the very outer Eastern suburbs of Melbourne. That was where I was born soon after. It was a hard birth; mum was still in shock and wasn't able to breathe or push very well. There were indications that I may been have deprived of oxygen, but who knows? I think my brain is pretty good.

My birth, so soon after grandfather's tragic death, pushed my mum and dad to their breaking point.

Nana didn't seem to have much luck with husbands. Her first husband, my mum's real dad, left his wife and two-year-old daughter to join the English navy in 1946. After she lost her second husband so tragically, she wasn't much help to my mum or her newborn. Mum did her best, but only managed to breast-feed me for one day, which may explain my many sensitivities to food.

Mum had to cope with her grief while caring for her newborn, my one-year-old sister, and our two-year-old brother. Another brother was born four years later and than another sister after four more years. Mum now had five children under the age of ten. Little ole me was stuck in the middle with an older brother and sister and a younger brother and sister, which sounds pretty good, but I often felt like the meat in a sandwich.

We lived in "the bush" east of Melbourne for another six years. "Bush" is iconic of Australia and can mean a couple of things. In this case, it's referring to the landscape: shrubs and bushes growing under a sparse canopy of eucalyptus-gum trees.

By 1964, our area had just started to develop. Mum and dad loved the new Mooroolbark housing estate, a lovely leafy suburb at the base of the Dandenong Ranges, the closest mountains to Melbourne. Although Mooroolbark was well equipped with shops and schools and close to the local train station, it was the local possums, kookaburras, beautiful magpies, lorikeets, and eastern rosellas that made living in the bush so enjoyable.

My dad was a very talented bricky (bricklayer) and had a great business going that he had built from scratch. He had a couple of blokes working for him while mum kept the books and looked after us kids. We were quite well off and lacked for nothing financially, although dad was a heavy drinker.

Peter, now my husband, grew up in the small mining town of Morawa, in the Mid West region of Western Australia, 3,500 kilometres away. Peter's family moved to Morawa in 1966 when his dad was hired as foreman at the Koolanooka Hills iron ore mine. He worked there for eight years.

I consider Morawa a mining town, but it also supports farms raising wheat, sheep, cattle, and sandalwood. Since 1962, the population has dropped from a couple of thousand to about 600. Like much of the "wheat belt" in Western Australia, the town is often in a period of drought.

Great swaths of land in Western Australia have been cleared to grow wheat, leaving only feral pests and weeds in abundance, and only a few hardy trees can survive summer temperatures that reach forty-eight degrees Celsius. The local desert, with annual rainfall averaging just over 300 millimetres, provides a sharp contrast to the beautiful bush where I lived, and where the Dandenong Ranges average more than twice as much rain and even occasional snowfall.

Peter was the oldest child to parents who had desperately tried for many years to have children. He was followed four years later by his only brother. Peter was surrounded by the desert and had a lot of freedom. At age ten he roamed the vast countryside on his bike and often went shooting rabbits with his dad and brother.

In 1974 the mine in Morawa closed and Peter's family moved across the country to the isolated settlement of Greenvale, Queensland, where his father was hired at the nickel mine. Greenvale is about 220 kilometres inland from the east coast of Australia, in the middle of bloody nowhere. It was purpose-built to house the local miners and their families; the only non-miners were a few shopkeepers who ran the general store and post office.

The train depot that served Greenvale was the site of the Three Rivers Hotel, which was made famous by Slim Dusty in the song of the same name written by Stan Coster. Peter remembers very fondly roaming the countryside on his motor bike, alone or with his mates, often shooting wild boars. Peter's free-roaming independence was shaped by the freedom of his life in Greenvale, especially during his first year there and then later on school holidays. To no one's surprise, in 1983, Peter moved to Perth and joined Australia's Elite Army Corps, the Special Air Service Regiment (SASR) at the age of twenty-one.

The biggest difference between Peter and I was that I grew up with a dad who was an abusive and violent alcoholic. As a child I had to be as tough as nails to survive the first six years of my life. That gave me a solid foundation that I didn't fully appreciate or become aware of until, at age thirty-three, I had my third daughter Avelynn and saw her fight for her life in the ICU when she was nine weeks old. Only then did I fully appreciate the strength of my character, and how my background shaped me into the person I am today. Ironically, my dad's abuse made me stronger.

My older brother, sister, and I were all very frightened of our dad—especially me. For some reason dad had it in for me, picked on me, and incessantly victimised me. He was often cruel. My father abused the love and trust I had for him as a baby and I learnt to be very wary and afraid of him. I often thought he might kill me.

I learnt to live. Not only with the fear, but also the fighting, yelling, screaming, and the victimisation. All of the craziness that came from living with a rampaging alcoholic, who was totally off his face with booze, anger, and apparent hatred. He was wasn't much better sober; I had to be constantly on guard when he was around. I remember that for the first six years of my life, I was being completely terrified of him and what he might do to me.

Dad would often mash my face into my food when I wouldn't eat. I remember being locked outside late at night in freezing cold; bashing on the front door begging for someone to let me in. Crying my eyes out and being so terrified of the dark when no one came. To a small child, this seemed like an eternity. Or hiding under my oldest brother's bed at night when he was asleep so my Dad wouldn't know where to find me when he came looking for me (as he often did.) My sister and I had our bare backsides beaten with his thick leather belt for daring to have fun and jumping on the our beds. Most of all it was living with the fear of the unknown and unpredictability of an alcoholic.

Even when I wasn't in the fight, I could hear it. I would lie in bed at night, stiff as a board, too scared to go to sleep. Always waiting for the sound of his footsteps in the hall that meant I was in trouble again, for nothing, for just being me. Living with the insecurity that even at night I wasn't safe and wasn't left alone.

Time and again my older brother, sister, and I were ordered out of bed in the wee hours of morning when I was three, four, or five and told to get into our best clothes (party dresses for my sister and me) so we would look "presentable." Dad would drive us to his mum's place. We called our grandmother "Franny." When my brother was little he couldn't say "granny," and the name stuck. Franny would phone dad, demanding that he bring us over so her friends could meet us, check us out, and congratulate her on what wonderful grandchildren she had.

Of course, we weren't interested in talking to Franny's buddies or my dad, who were all drinking, smoking, and playing loud music. We just wanted to be left alone, not rudely woken up and forced to talk to these adults, who were often strangers.

We had no say in the matter, so off we'd go. I remember coping by staring at an amazing piece of art Franny had hung on the wall above her kitchen table. It was an intricate pattern of swirls made by thousands of nails and cotton woven around them in amazing colours. I used to get lost in the swirls and the beautiful colours that descended down and up and pretended I was running around the swirls trying to find the beginning and end of them.

Often we came home with cigarette burns on our best dresses. Of course mum would have a hell of a day with us as we'd be exhausted from lack of sleep but high on sugar from lollies and lemonade. These visits to Franny's were one of my mum's recurring nightmares.

Dad was very fond of his .22-calibre rifle and often terrified us by waving it around and pretending he was going to kill us and mum. We were just small children and never knew if he was serious. He placed the rifle hard against mum's head a couple of times and told us, "Say good-bye to your mummy kids, she's going to die." Another time, he shot at mum as she was running away; he missed her but shot through our neighbour kid's bedroom window. Thankfully, no one was hurt.

As a child of a violent and abusive alcoholic, I learnt to be exceptionally careful around dad in what I said and in how I behaved. I developed a razor sharp ability to pick up any feelings within the family when he was around. I learnt to listen to how he drove up to the house and shut the car door. If he drove in fast and came to an abrupt halt and then quickly slammed the door shut, I knew he was in a bad mood. If dad parked the car gently and just closed the door then his mood would generally be okay.

I learnt to listen for the sound of his footsteps. The way he walked was another indicator of what mood he was in, and whether or not I was in for more abuse. Basically, I learnt to become invisible and to not draw any attention. I gradually developed an sixth sense of how to read body language and the general mood of the environment in order to protect myself from him.

Dad would sometimes ask me to help make St Kilda sandwiches—named after his favourite Aussie rules football team—with peanut butter for the white, Vegemite for the black, and strawberry jam for the red. Even when he was being nice, I could never trust that he wouldn't backhand me because I was going too slowly, or making too much of a mess, or just not doing it the way he expected of me. I could never relax when I was around dad or if he was in the house. I certainly could never trust him.

I wet the bed until the age of nine. Though my mum was great and supported me, it was humiliating for me and another thing my dad would torment me about. I had a star chart to remind me that if I went for three or four nights without wetting the bed, I would be rewarded. Wow, somehow that didn't work out as my bed-wetting had a lot to do with feeling extremely insecure and anxious. It may have been partly hereditary, but it was just another part of my myself that I hated, and beat myself up about.

I can vividly remember my Nana (when I was nine) trying to wake me up when she stayed over at our place, trying to get me to go to the loo. I wasn't happy about being woken up and was tried to punch her and fight her off. Hopefully she has since forgiven me. Bed-wetting wasn't the only problem I had, but it helped convince me I was never good enough. I thought I was completely dumb, and I often wondered what I was doing on the earth and why I had been born at all.

I suffered from very low self esteem and lacked confidence in social situations. I cringed at the slightest threat, and was torn between wishing I would just up and die, and fighting to stay alive. I simply wasn't allowed to be me, as I often had to switch off my feelings and my needs in order to get what care was available for me at the time. If I hurt somewhere or fell over, I learnt to deal with the pain and not complain; to do nothing that would draw attention.

I remember running down the road with my dad as we walked to a fish 'n' chips shop. I fell over and took a chunk out of my knee. I was screaming as the blood was rushing down my leg, and dad didn't even help me. When we got to the shop, he sat me on the shelf, and I wasn't allowed to move. I walked back home and realized "quick smart" that crying didn't get me anywhere. So I learnt to care for and nurture myself. I also learnt that I wasn't special and unique, or worthy of love, or to have trust in my environment, or to rely on my parents for my basic needs, or trust that my mum would be around to care for, protect, and nurture me, as my dad so often threatened to kill her.

Unfortunately, many times my brother, sister, and I saw our dad, who had a black belt in karate, physically abuse our mum. Once my older brother phoned grandmother Franny to come and save my mum- as dad was slashing at her stomach, while she was jumping out of the way. Meanwhile, my brother was trying his best to protect my sister and me by holding onto the handle of the door that separated the lounge from the hallway where we were hiding, trying to be brave for our mum.

Fortunately, Franny arrived in time. Unfortunately, dad slashed Franny in the stomach when she positioned herself in front of mum to protect her from dad's drunken rage. There were many more things like this happened to mum.

Dad often said he wished I wasn't around, and I thought he might one day try to kill me. Life wasn't much fun when he was around, though I can remember having fun playing with my cat and swimming outside in our small pool. I learnt to be a very resilient child, but one that certainly didn't have her needs met.

When I was as young as eight months, dad would say, "Come to Daddy, Michelle, come on, come to Daddy," and I would very warily crawl to him. But when I reached him, he would push me away, and say, "Gee's you are useless!" Or, "I don't really want you!" Or simply push me away with disgust on his face.

Of course mum had tried to leave dad on many occasions. I remember driving around the local suburbs in the dark with the frightened faces of my sister and brother looking back at me in the dim light. We drove around waiting for my dad to get over his drunken rage. Occasionally we'd go to some shelter or stay over at my Nana's house (my mum's mum). But the strong pull was there that always led her back to my dad. In those days, there was no support for battered women and their children as there is today.

Mum had been separated from dad for over a year, and he had been under psychiatrist care for several months. He appeared to have his problems under control, especially his temper and drinking. So mum made a decision to let him back into our lives, because she loved him and he loved her. That decision nearly cost us our lives.

It was February 1973 and I was six. I had settled comfortably into my first two weeks at the local primary school. I remember having so much fun with a couple of nice friends, swinging on the monkey bars. I was happy to be at school and felt so grown up.

My joy was short-lived, and the day nearly ended in tragedy. This time was different, and mum finally left dad for good. Approximately three weeks after he'd moved back in, mum went to our school for teacher-parent interviews. As a show of trust in my dad, mum decided my older brother, sister, and I could safely be left home with him to look after us.

When mum returned home, something just snapped in dad's brain. Mum said she never knew what it was, but dad was determined that mum wasn't allowed to live any longer, nor were we! He was screaming at us, "You all have to die!" He staggered into their bedroom and got his loaded rifle from its hiding place. We heard his heavy footsteps coming towards us in the lounge room. He started shooting at us, but he was so drunk that he missed. He kept shooting as we ran screaming around the lounge in panic and terror. Mum was screaming at us, trying to protect us, and finally managed to shepherd us behind her, protecting us with her body, and giving us a chance to escape.

But God or providence was finally smiling down and protecting us. Mum handed four-month-old Adam to seven-year-old Rowan and told him to run like blazes to the car with Sharon and me behind him in hot pursuit. Mum remembers that we backed out of the door trying not to make it look obvious that we were disappearing. Once out of the door, we turned around and ran to the car. Mum followed—she always kept keys and lots of money hidden in the garden for just such an occasion. So we were able to escape and took off in the car while dad continued shooting at us.

Mum took off, revving the little VW as fast as it would go. I ducked down in the back, terrified that he was going to shoot me through the rear window. I thought I was going to die, and I couldn't believe the terror. Even now, thinking about that incident brings fear into my heart; I don't know how we escaped unscathed.

According to the police, after we'd left dad deliberately poured petrol all over the house, including our bedrooms, the lounge, the kitchen, our treasured childhood toys, and mum's beautiful crockery collection from her mum. He then blew up the gas heater by shooting it. It was obvious that it was arson by the random way the fire burnt parts of our bed and miraculously left my dolls house and jewellery box slightly scorched but intact. I still keep and protect that scorched jewellery box, but everything else I owned went up in flames.

Mum's brother, Uncle Geoff, received a frantic phone call from dad just before he set fire to our house. Geoff thought dad sounded like he'd lost his mind and drove over. Geoff lived forty minutes way and the house was nearly gone by the time he arrived. He found dad unconscious in the doorway and dragged him to safety before calling the fire department. The house was pretty much gutted, and nearly everything we owned was gone.

From a court hearing later, we learnt dad wanted to destroy everything in the house, reasoning that the courts would throw the book at him anyway for trying to shoot us. I think it finally dawned on him that mum wasn't coming back. If he wasn't getting anything from the house then neither would mum nor we kids. He had intended to destroy every single thing we valued or owned.

I don't remember anything about mum going to court or a court case but I do remember dad kind of disappearing from my life for a year or so. He went to prison after being found guilty of arson.

In 1972, Australia had enacted the single pension, so mum could afford to rent a small two-bedroom flat for us in Caulfield, an inner city suburb of Melbourne. We were poor and basically had nothing; nearly everything we owned burned with the house.

Thank God for the Salvation Army, who clothed us and fed us until mum could stand on her feet.

Some of our family members scrounged around and managed to find a couple of beds, mattresses, fridge, and a kitchen table for us—just the bare essentials. We didn't have a couch, but I can remember sitting on the floor watching cartoons on television, not really bothered by the lack of seating.

We had a cat called Shere Khan who really was a miracle. Somehow she had survived the house fire by getting up into the roof and was able to breath until she was rescued. She was never the same again. She frequently entertained us by jumping from our second story balcony. No matter how hard we tried to stop her, she always managed. Shere Khan was pretty wild after the fire.

After being so confined and restricted by our life with dad, when we moved to the flat, Rowen, Sharon, and I also were kind of wild. For the first time in my life there was no monster hanging over us, and I rejoiced in my freedom. We made firm friends with a couple of other kids in the flats and roamed our street seeing what mischief we could get up to. The car park was lots of fun, and my brother would often coax me into picking up dog poo and putting it on one of the tenant's cars whom we nicknamed Mr. Shitty, because he never said a nice word to us.

Yes, I am very sorry for doing that. A favourite trick of my brother and his friends was to pick up dog poo, put it in a paper bag, place it on one of the neighbours mats, knock on the door and when they heard footsteps, set it on fire. Of course, the unsuspecting person would stamp the fire out and step in the poo. My brother and his mates would watch the whole thing from their prearranged hiding place.

I wasn't involved with the flaming dog poo, but I would look for lollies or chewing gun on the ground that we used to pick up and eat or start chewing again. To this day I am not sure if I really needed to do this, but it certainly contributed to my very good immune system. Living in the flat was fun, though Sharon opted to eventually live with dad again as they developed a close relationship. Mum knew my sister loved him a lot. This didn't bother me all that much as my sister and I hadn't always got along that well. Dad picked on me and not her, so there was sibling rivalry between us.

Two years later mum met my soon-to-be step dad and we all moved to Kilsyth, an outer eastern suburb of Melbourne. This was close to where we had been bought up. There were only a few finished houses in the estate, so Rowen and I enjoyed ourselves immensely amongst the partly built houses, and sloshed around the puddles in our gumboots. Mum and step dad's wedding went smoothly; mum wore a fabulously gorgeous, bright pink, long wedding gown. Sharon continued to live with dad, but Rowen, Adam, and I enjoyed moving to our new house.

Although I had some fun, and enjoyed mucking around with my brothers, I had difficulty making friends at my new school. At seven, I had been through a lot and wasn't coping well.

I now had a step-dad, but I didn't want an adult male in my life. I was content without a dad and didn't feel the need for one. I was quite peeved that mum had remarried and never grew close to my step dad. To be fair to him he lived with his mother until he was thirty-three and married my mum. He wasn't equipped to handle four children that weren't particularly interested in ever again being told what to do by a male.

I wasn't emotionally equipped to handle these big changes, and the emotional stress and strain caught up with me. I just couldn't cope with life. Essentially, I had a nervous breakdown at the age of seven, which seems absurd, but it was true.

I started acting quite strangely when we went out in the car and would put my security blanket over my head. My theory was that if I couldn't see anyone then no one could see me. I also pretended I was a duck. Apparently I told my mum that people like ducks and ducks didn't talk, they quacked. So I quacked often when mum tried to talk to me. I didn't have any friends, played by myself at lunch time, sulked a lot, spent a lot of time in my bedroom, and closed down emotionally.

I saw a psychiatrist who tried very hard to discover why I wanted to be a duck and what was going on in my head. I remember seeing her and thought she was very safe and kind. I received therapy for a year. In that time I mostly played on a green mat with a make shift garden, toy house, and animals that I could choose such as dogs, cats, and birds.

I could also choose what family members were allowed to be on the mat to play. When the psychiatrist put 'the dad' on the mat, I always threw him against the wall as hard and as fast as I could, trying to break it in half or destroy it. At the end of the year that father figure was never allowed on the patch of green grass.

The psychologist said to mum, "Sorry, but Michelle's step dad doesn't know how to relate to her or your other children so don't ever expect them to be able to relate to him."

I loathed all adult males and was terrified and frightened of them. I wanted them to go away. My grade four teacher was no exception. When I entered the classroom with my mum to meet him, I saw his black moustache and ran screaming down the corridor as fast as I could. Mum hastily apologised and took off after me. The poor teacher never got over my reaction to him and for the two years I had him as a teacher he let me get away with blue murder.

In primary school, I continually struggled to read, write, spell, do math, and generally cope with learning. I was constantly bullied. I hated school with a passion, but remembered that I had also been bullied back at my school in Caulfield. On one occasion, as I went to enter the girls toilet, a few boys from my class picked me up and dumped me in the bin telling me, "You're a boy not a girl, you aren't allowed to use the girls toilet!"

I wasn't able to relate to my peers or trust anyone. I learnt early not to rely on anyone else and not to look to anyone for help when I had a problem. From an early age, I learnt to solve my own problems. I never told my mum about the bullying, but after years of it eventually learnt to hit back.

Except for how to hit bullies, I didn't learn much in primary school. Looking back, perhaps I had a learning disability or auditory processing disorder (APD) like my daughter. Avelynn also has dyslexia and learning disabilities from a stroke at nine weeks.

APD can be difficult to detect, particularly in children. Children with APD have trouble distinguishing subtle differences between spoken words. Something interferes with processing and interpreting auditory information. A child suffering from APD often misinterprets word sounds, making conversations difficult. Background noise aggravates the problem.

If a teacher says, "Tell me how a couch and a chair are alike," the child with APD may hear, "Tell me how a cow and a hair are alike." APD is often associated with dyslexia, attention deficit disorder, autism spectrum disorders, specific language impairments, or developmental delay.

Although I was never officially diagnosed with a learning impairment, developmental delay, or APD, school was a major challenge for me. My grade three teacher literally gave up teaching me and instead let me play with blocks on the mat. She told my mum, "Sorry, but Michelle can't seem to learn anything and is beyond teaching,. I don't know what to do with her."

I remember trying to figure out, for example, what "ie," "ar," and "ur" were. For the life of me, I couldn't figure out if they were sounds or where I was supposed to put them in a word. Mum decided the best course of action—after repeatedly calling the class room teacher inadequate because she couldn't teach me—was to take me out of school until there was a different teacher or a new school year. I stayed home and watched "Sesame Street." No wonder children love the show, it's so much fun!

Six months later I went back to school. Though I had learnt some things from Sesame Street—especially Big Bird—I hadn't quite caught up to my peers. Learning continued to be a big problem and further lowered self-esteem. To cope with how inadequate I felt academically, I became the class clown.

I never answered a question or took part of classroom discussions in case I misheard what was being discussed. I didn't want to look like a fool. I needed to feel secure and safe, to be where there was no chance of being ridiculed or verbally abused. I unconsciously learnt to avoid situations where I was exposed to ridicule; the pain was still raw and I could not have borne any more. Strangely, no one connected my learning and classroom behaviour to the traumas of my early childhood.

I'd often hear mum and my teachers talking, suggesting that I would be better off going to a "special school" for my high school years. Those schools are typically for children with low IQs, but mine was never officially tested. They thought I wouldn't cope with high school and would not amount to anything. They were trying their best for me.

Unsurprisingly, I also never thought I'd amount to anything or do anything significant with my life. The only aspiration I had, from age nine, was to travel to the UK some day so that I could check out where my grandparents and ancestors had come from. I did go, twelve years later, but that's another story!

Whilst fighting my own demons and trying to prepare for high school, another story unfolded alongside mine and profoundly affected me.

My older sister, Sharon, had spent many years yo-yoing between our house and dad's. When I was in grade five, she decided once and for all to come and live with us. Her life had become unbearable at dad's. His alcoholism was profoundly affecting his relationship with Fay (our step mum) and their three children. My step-sister Shelly was Fay's child from a previous marriage, and I had two half-sisters, Susie and Tania.

Sharon had practically raised Susie and Tania as her own, and I knew them fairly well. I often stayed overnight or weekends at their place. Fay, was a well-meaning and nice-enough woman, but very frightened and anxious from dad's brutal abuse. Fay became too despondent to manage basic mothering and household responsiblities.

At age ten, Sharon took over, cooking, ironing, and cleaning. She was also a surrogate mum to our sisters. Susie and Tania gave Sharon's life meaning and were a source of great happiness; they became exceptionally close.

When I was in grade six, and Sharon was in her first year of high school, things improved briefly. My mum had taught Fay how to save money without dad knowing. Money was one way he kept her trapped and dependent within their destructive relationship, keeping tight control over their finances and bank account. With mum's encouragement, Fay, Susie, and Tania eventually escaped to Queensland, and Sharon came to live with us permanently.

I didn't spend much time thinking about Fay, Susie, and Tania, who were then four and two. I was happily anticipating the end of primary school and to joining Rowen and Sharon at the local high school. One day in September, when I was getting excited about buying high school books, mum seemed a little sad, and I knew something wasn't right. She asked Sharon and me to sit down on the couch in the lounge because she had something important to tell us.

Sharon and I exchanged glances because we knew this was serious. "Okay, girls," mum said, "This is not going to be easy; I've had some bad news. Fay, Susie, and Tania went for a drive with a friend up in Queensland and were hit head-on by a semi-trailer that was on the wrong side of the road."

I glanced at Sharon to see how she was taking the news—she didn't look good. I remember hoping with all my might that mum was telling us a horrible, made-up nightmare and that I could take the words back. I knew how much Susie and Tania meant to Sharon, and I wished it was me in the crash. If I could have, I would have taken the place of those girls for Sharon. They were her life.

Mum kept talking even though I could see she was uncomfortable and worried about telling us the rest of the story. I didn't want to hear anymore—I just wanted her to shut up!

"Unfortunately," mum continued, "Susie, Tania and Fay were not wearing seat belts; they all went through the windscreen. Susie is still in hospital with massive brain injuries, but the doctors think she will be okay. Tania was killed instantly and Fay died twenty minutes later in hospital."

Sharon's grief was palpable; she fell off the couch screaming, "Arrrr! No! No!" Mum hugged us both, and we hugged each other. I wanted to be the one to die, to be in that car—not Susie and Tania! I wanted to take Sharon's pain away. She loved Susie and Tania, more like her children than sisters. Sharon was the one who washed and ironed their clothes, packed their lunches, and cuddled them when they needed cuddling. Sharon was the one who dried their tears and was there for them when Fay couldn't.

It was a tragic twist of fate that sent Fay from terror to freedom, and then to her death. It's not that I didn't love my sister's (and Fay too, in my own way) it's just that I wasn't bought up with them. In the short time they had been around, it was always my sister Sharon that kept them safe.

Because I wasn't as upset as Sharon, I thought their deaths didn't affect me as much. But I just buried the feelings I didn't know how to manage, like every trauma in my life. I became expert at burying feelings when I didn't know what to do with them. I was already coping with so much, I buried my grief deep down where I thought it was safe and would never affect me.

Sadly, we weren't even invited to Fay's and Tania's funerals and never learnt where they were buried. Our feelings were discounted, and we were kind of expected to "just get over them," which was pretty harsh. It was especially hard for Sharon, because she had an amazing connection with them. Sharon and I never spoke again of Fay, Tania, or grandmother Franny until we were adults; it just hurt too much.

After the car accident Franny (dad's mum) raised Susie and we only saw her once. I never saw Franny again, but I don't know why. Maybe mum and Franny never got along that well, or maybe Franny decided to sever her ties with Sharon and me so that Susie could heal without yo-yoing between us.

I know it was better for Susie to be in Franny's care rather than our dad's. He had enough trouble looking after himself and his alcoholism was running rampant. I have often wondered why I never saw Franny again. I did love her and she usually had my best interest at heart; she had saved us from dad a few times.

I also often thought of Susie and how she turned out. You know: what she looked like, did she ever think of us, did she recover from her brain injury to live a fulfilling life? It wasn't fair for Sharon and me to never see Franny or Susie. Once again I buried my grief somewhere safe to cope with later. I can still see Susie in my mind's eye.

When she came out of hospital, she paid us a very quick visit. I tried to talk to her, but she sounded funny and didn't seem to know what was going on. Her hair was extremely short, and I could see scars all over her head where she had been stitched up after going through the windscreen. She didn't stay long, as she was tired, and that was the only time that I saw her. That visit might have been the end of the story except for an ironic twist of fate in 1993, fifteen years later.

I was sharing a house with three others in Glen Waverley, east of Melbourne. One day, we were in the kitchen, chatting about where we had lived and how many siblings we had. I mentioned that I hadn't seen one of my sisters for fifteen years and wondered what had happened to her.

Something about the way I said it made one of my mates ask what her surname was. When I told him, he said a friend of his knew someone with her name who was "a bit simple" and couldn't talk properly. It was Susie! How incredible! The chances were so unlikely of finding one of the few people who knew our sister and having a conversation about our siblings was miraculous.

Finally, Sharon and I learned what happened to our sister Susie. Sharon was excited about the prospect of seeing her again and got her phone numbers, etc. On the other hand, I had buried my feelings so deeply, that I told myself I didn't miss Susie. After all, it had been fifteen years! I had no inclination to see her again.

Sharon eventually tracked Susie down; she had married and was living in Adelaide, the capitol of South Australia. Like the rest of us, Susie absolutely adored cats and owned a couple. Mum, my sisters, and I are cat crazy. Our beloved cats can get away with absolutely anything: wrecking havoc with their claws, smashing breakables, and sleeping with us. We thoroughly pamper and spoil our cats, paying large vet bills, and over-spending on food. Just a wee bit obsessed!

While writing this book, I've read articles that helped me understand the language and feelings that defined what happened to Sharon and me. I can begin to gain some mastery over those experiences. I can clearly see that I buried my feelings. Typically, people who have lost a sibling are not afraid to be with others who are grieving.

I have read that bereaved siblings are often unable to help themselves with grief. They have been so hurt and become so vulnerable that they cannot tolerate their own feelings. They want to disown their own vulnerability and instead project their feelings onto others who are grieving, and then take care of that other person.

Learning to accept my own vulnerability has been a hard lesson. It is hard to accept that people you knew died in car accidents, especially when they are your sister and step mum. After all, I was three months shy of my twelfth birthday and it was easier for me to go numb instead of dealing with the grief associated with such a horrific loss.

We never had any counselling, and we were masters of pretence. If you didn't show that you hurt inside, and you cover your true feelings with smiles and by acting the clown, all was well, wasn't it? Sharon and I had been well programmed not to show what was really going on inside us. Our older brother, Rowen, was an expert as well. What was the point of complaining? All appeared well with us emotionally; we learnt to bury our feelings and get on with life.

During all of my childhood and most of my adult life, I disowned my feelings. I hardly knew what made me tick, or why I did certain things or react certain ways. I much preferred to take care of other people. I never knew that burying my feelings was a typical outcome of sibling loss, and maybe also typical of having an abusive, alcoholic parent. I naively thought that if I didn't acknowledge my feelings, then they just didn't exist. I did not realize that my feelings continued to fester, building hurt layer upon layer, taking me farther away from myself.

I became such a master at burying my feelings that only during the last couple of years have I honestly looked at what and who I am. Only recently have I taken the time to acknowledge what I have been through—this is where my wonderful daughter, Avelynn, has been such a benefit to me.

Chapter 2

Emotional Chaos

Avelynn is a reflection, because she highlights my loss of my sisters' and my stepmum's companionship. Avelynn came so close to dying so many times that I had to admit to myself that Ayla and Kara might lose their sister, just as I had. This realization forced me to face my own vulnerability.

At the time, I was never sure why I was so adamant about Ayla and Kara being in the ICU with Avelynn when she was nine weeks old. It's obvious now. I was ensuring that if Avelynn died her sister's would not be left out and would have people around so that they could cope with such a profound loss. Only since I have started writing this do I understand the connection. Losing Tania and Fay, and virtually losing Susie, made me realise life would never be the same again but became more real, and I became more careful. I ensure my children always wear seat belts because I know they might die without them. Sometimes, paranoia works.

After primary school, I learnt anew to bury my grief and sorrow and get on with life. We had no counselling and learnt not to speak about what happened within our family, although Sharon and I carried the scars.

High school was tough, especially the first year. Rowen and Sharon were one and two years ahead of me and had promised me a "royal flush" as an induction to high school: having my head flushed down the toilet. For a few months I was scared this would happen before I realised it was a hoax.

I managed to fight off a couple of bullies who thought I was ripe for picking. By then I was a tough character, though I often didn't show just how outraged, angry, or upset I really was. These emotions bubbled just beneath the surface. I did manage to pass most of my subjects, although not brilliantly, and I even managed a few laughs with some friends from primary school.

Another major disruption occurred during my first year of high school. It was in October 1979, two months before my thirteenth birthday. It seemed that my family couldn't avoid the cataclysm that surrounded dad's alcoholism.

Dad had a unfortunate upbringing and drank to avoid painful feelings. He tried to control his outrageous temper and sought help from Alcoholics Anonymous (AA) to understand and improve his life. AA has helped many people but, tragically, it couldn't help dad. With the loss of Fay and their children, his alcoholism became uncontrollable. He had nothing to stand on, no way of dealing with his feelings, and thought no one could help him.

Dad turned back to abusing mum, demanded that Sharon be handed over to him, because it was his right to have his daughter back. He was determined to keep hounding mum. During the months before that fateful day in October, mum had received so many abusive phone calls from dad that she was scared to answer the phone.

We were all on tender hooks. My step-dad was scared shitless and wasn't going to be anyone's hero. Mum hid the hounding from us, and I was oblivious. I expended most of my energy trying to concentrate on my school work and to deal with the bullying. Typically, mum tried shield us from her worries. Not until they started to escalate did I realise just how worried mum really was.

One night, mum was worried that dad would come to our home and physically take Sharon. Mum had arranged for Sharon to have a sleep-over at a friend's. My older brother, Rowen, went to Venturers (scouts) as usual while my younger brother, sister, and I slept at home.

About the time mum expected Rowen home from Venturers, she heard a car pulling up out the front. She heard the car door slam, and then footsteps on the front path. There was a "family knock" on the door, the one we all used to let mum know it wasn't a stranger. Unfortunately, it was dad, who had learned our secret knock.

I was asleep, but I learned bits and pieces of what transpired next. Mum tried to shut the door to stop him from coming in, but it was to no avail. He was extremely strong and broke the safety chain, forcing his way into our house. Mum was horrified that he was in our house and roaring drunk. The commotion, only metres away from my bed, woke me instantly.

Although I have blocked out a lot of what happened that night, I clearly remember my dad yelling threats at mum and step dad, "I swore to myself, if any man ever took my family off me I would kill him!" There was so much screaming going on. I tried plugging my ears so I could stop listening. I was extremely frightened of all the yelling that was taking place and was crying to myself.

I remember thinking, "I had better save myself! I'll quickly put my set of drawers against the door so no one can get me." I heaved and pulled my heavy draws in front of my bedroom door. Thinking I was safe, I must have slept for a little while.

I awoke to the sound of someone running down the hallway past my room and then back again. Suddenly, I heard two extremely loud gunshots —right in front of my door. I screamed in absolute mind numbing terror, glad of the set of drawers that were blocking the entrance to my room. I remember screaming and screaming, then thought; "Oh my God! Whoever it is, knows I am in my room! I might be next! What if he or she comes after me with the gun? Who's going to save me?"

After what seemed like an eternity, listening carefully for any threatening footsteps, or floor boards creaking under the heavy white carpet, I decided to open my bedroom door. I reasoned to myself that since I hadn't heard anyone outside my room, I should be okay.

With trepidation and an absolute sense of foreboding, I slowly opened my bedroom door after once again pulling and pushing the heavy drawers away. I was ready to defend myself from attack at any moment, though I was shaking uncontrollably. I don't know what I would have done if I had been attacked. I tried to look everywhere at once.

Seeing no one, I crept out my door into the hallway. My cat, Momotaro, was sitting on the mat in the lounge room, waiting for me. As I walked across to the lounge room I looked left and saw dad's slumped body. Sobbing uncontrollably, I ran to my cat, grabbing him and holding on to him for dear life, as if he held the key to my sanity, but knowing that I had to walk back into the hallway.

Excruciatingly slowly, I made my way along the hallway and stopped about one metre from my dad. Painfully I crept closer to him. I could only see half of his body—the other half was obscured by a bend in the wall—trying to figure out why he was lying down. I could see his legs, and noticed that he had bare feet, which I thought strange.

Drawing on courage of a type that I'd never had to show before, never even knew that I had, I walked over to him—incredibly close—but I never touched him. As I leant over him, I saw that he wasn't moving. It was surreal; it was difficult; but I had to see his whole body. I didn't check his pulse; I never thought about doing that. I had just wanted to see why he was lying down on his stomach.

My brain wasn't working and I hadn't connected the gun shots to him lying down. For some reason, I thought he'd get back up and come after me. Even then, I was afraid that he would jump up and get me. I didn't want to be alone with him in the hall way. Thank goodness, I still held my cat close to my chest for comfort. I still couldn't see anyone else that could help me. As my eyes travelled from his bare feet to his head, I finally saw the blood. His red blood contrasted strongly with our painted white walls; his blood was smeared broadly all the way down the wall, from chest height all the way down and into our white, shag-pile carpet.

Fear temporarily immobilized me for those couple of seconds, and to this day I have a picture of his body in my brain, with the blood-smeared wall on the left-hand side of our hall way. It's a snap shot of my last time with him, frozen in time. I don't want that picture in my brain.

Screaming hysterically, I ran back into my room, shutting the door and trying to shut out what I had seen. It could have been minutes or hours later when someone came into my room, told me to shut up and look after my eight-year-old sister. I remember falling asleep cuddling my precious little sister and my cat.

I woke up later that night to camera flashes that penetrated under the door to my room. I heard lots of voices, and one time I stuck my head out of the door only to be told by a police man to shut it again. But I sneaked another look and saw a stretcher with a body on it going out the door. I presumed it was dad, though I had not been told he was dead. I learned the next day that dad was dead, and my step dad had been rushed to hospital with a suspected heart attack.

Whatever happened next is only a blur. Mum was charged with killing dad, but got off on self defence after years of court cases. She only spent one night in prison. I never knew much about that, or even if she was ever officially charged with manslaughter. After a hectic week spending most nights at my uncle and auntie's place we kids went back to school as if nothing happened. I really can't remember anything else.

My friends said I never spoke about what happened, and it appeared that I just got on with my life. The reality was that I was a master at hiding my feelings and probably wouldn't have known what I felt. Once again we kids never received counselling. Amazingly, I have never spoken about my dad's death, and writing about it has been hard.

I am glad I have finally shared this horrific experience. This is what happens at the extreme end of domestic violence. It's not pretty, and there are other children and women who have been killed by their fathers or husbands and a smaller group that have been killed by their mother or wife. I know I am among the children who witnessed the killing of a parent—though only the sound of it—but I consider myself one of the lucky ones. That night could have turned out a lot worse. My friends and relations could have read how our family were slain by my father.

Understanding the hideous affects of alcoholism and its effects has been an interest of mine. Is it an interest of yours? Is there someone you know who drinks? Do you drink? Alcoholism is an addiction—but I am not into the blame game.

Yes, dad drank to his ultimate oblivion—but he drank for a reason. It wasn't until I was twenty-five and went to Al-Anon—a recovery group for those who have been affected by someone else's drinking—that I finally understood that if and when you take away the alcohol that person still has the "ism's". What are they? They are the reason the person started drinking. I found some peace and answers in Al-Anon, mainly that alcoholism is a disease, and I try my best to understand it.

Sure, I used to think it's not fair, Why did I have to go through all that physical and emotional abuse? What was the point to my life? Why didn't my mum leave him? Why did he kill our animals, break my mum's bones, lock me outside at night, and terrorise me? Was it really only the alcohol? Why did he seem to not really care?

I can't answer every question but I do know that looking at life from a one-sided perspective isn't right or fair either. There are many reasons my dad was like that. He also came from a broken family with abuse and alcoholism. His mum was a single mother trying to do the best she could, as she had him when she was sixteen. His dad didn't hang around for long, and my dad was brought up in several different pubs. He had several surrogate dads, so I suppose he too learnt to survive with the best he had at hand, as my grandmother Franny did.

Society says dad was wrong, and he was. I don't condone what he did, but at the end of the day, blaming others for your problems or where you find yourself doesn't solve anything. I still don't understand all the things that he did, and I am sure he didn't either. I like to think if he'd been shown another way, or learnt to control his anger and where it came, from he might have been different.

Ironically, mum and dad were the best teachers I ever had. I thank both of them for shaping me into who I am today; someone that can cope with rain or shine, happy or sad, angry or calm, health or disease. I didn't appreciate my upbringing during my tough times, but I'm now tough as bricks. Without my background, I often wonder how I would have coped with Avelynn, and what she's been given to deal with. Maybe one day, Avelynn's condition will change, and I only hope I have the love, wisdom, courage, and gratitude to make my way. So thank you, mum and dad, for making me this way; I wish you know how I feel about you both today. Especially you, dad. Although you've passed away, I know you would be proud of me

I have been driven over the years to learn why dad was an abusive alcoholic, and I have learnt a lot. Some of which I'd like to share, knowing that I may help someone. It was tragic and pointless for my dad's life to end as it did; it could have been prevented. What I'd like to share is a letter I wrote to dad the other day.

> Dear Dad,
>
> I know you were a raging alcoholic. Verbally abusive, often cruel and vindictive—but I also know that you loved with as much intensity as you hated. Yes, you raged, and the alcohol didn't help. You had extreme emotions that you projected into your family. You raged when you reacted strongly to emotions—the emotions you felt when we pressed your buttons.

> You raged out of feelings of fear, sadness, shame, inadequacy, guilt, and loss. People tried to help you, but really no one could give you the help and support you needed. I've always thought it was such a shame you couldn't be stronger and overcome your weaknesses of rage and alcohol abuse. You were never shown how to express your anger in a healthy way. Instead, it was repressed, stuffed down and ignored from your childhood and the way your parents treated you.
>
> Your anger created a wealth of resentment, mental, and emotional problems. You stuffed down those feelings of shame, anger, guilt, isolation, fear, and sadness so much you were a volcano waiting to erupt. Erupt you did—into my life. You helped shape the strong person I am today, but not without a lot of heartache, anguish and misery especially throughout my teenage years. Dad, how I'd wished it could have ended better for you! My last image of you was being wheeled away in a body bag.

After dad died, I went back to school like nothing had happened and passed year seven without any more hiccups, celebrating my thirteenth birthday in late December. The rest of my early-to-mid teenage years are a reflection of what many children of alcoholics, or those with codependent behaviours learnt from childhood, go through. Liz Byrski writes in *Under The Influence* ,

> Children raised in alcoholic families, like many of the spouses of alcoholics, view the world through the eyes of a victim, experiencing feelings of powerlessness which trap them often well into their adult lives. They have a tendency to live their lives through others by compulsively involving themselves in relationships with people whom they think they can change. This may result in subtle manipulation, deviousness, and authoritarianism. Whatever the behaviour, because their highs are achieved through the good behaviour of others over

> whom they are powerless, they are programmed for self-destruction.

By sixteen, I was programmed for self-destruction. I'd survived so much, but underneath was a simmering volcano ready to erupt at the slightest friction. I'd been going out with Mitchell and I lived my life through him, just as Liz Byrski described. I compulsively involved myself in his life, his friends, his feelings, thinking that I could change him. When he was happy, I was happy. When he was sad, angry, or accepting, then I was also. My feelings reflected his, and I was on a mission of self-destruction. He often lied, cheated on me, and ordered me around like I was his slave. I always put up with it; deep down I thought I deserved it and was lucky to have a boyfriend. Plus, I thought I wouldn't find anyone else to love me.

We shared lots of highs, alternating with abysmal lows. My self-esteem, already fragile, took a lot of blows in direct proportion to how Mitchell treated me. I covered up my grief, sadness, and inadequacy with a forced fake clown mask. I played the idiot, including many drunken episodes, fooling around dancing the 'Hokey Pokey' on a car roof. I thought I was invincible until I sobered up, massively depressed.

Mitchell was one of only a couple of boyfriends, and with each I followed the same relationship patterns for which I was programmed. Few people, even my own family, realised my torment. I certainly never spoke of it or connected my behaviour and depression to the physiological effects of growing up as I did. I found it very difficult to talk about my feelings and my upbringing, even with a well meaning social worker. I felt no one would understand anyway so what was the use? I thought I had to pretend all was well with me, that I could cope and not reveal my true self, because I felt people wouldn't like or accept me if they knew what I was really like or what I thought.

I never really acknowledged my accomplishments or saw myself properly. I didn't know my strengths or weaknesses, basically just accepted what had been dad's low opinion of me and carried that through my teen years. I felt dumb, stupid, clumsy, shy, a failure, unimportant, so my feelings didn't count. My low self-esteem was manifested as lack of assertiveness in my relationships. I felt unable to ask for what I wanted lest they stopped loving me.

On the other hand, if a relationship didn't matter to me, then I would tell them off. A couple of girls bullied me at school and I nearly had a fight with one. But I didn't crave their acceptance or love, so I didn't care.

My grief and sadness, the bullying, trying unsuccessfully to excel in academics, trying to keep up my cheerful mask, my background, and the underlying issues from dad's alcoholism, abuse, and death eventually took their toll. I felt angry and out of control. I was angry a lot; anger was how I coped when life didn't seem fair, and I had never learnt how to cope with my anger or sadness.

My friends didn't quite get this, and neither did my mum, who thought I was a bit of a bitch. Maybe I was. I didn't think the social worker would understand my background, and I was too ashamed to talk about dad and how he died. I alternated between depression and acting out.

The only times I felt close to normal were walking the dog or cuddling my cat. I actually enjoyed what I was learning from one of my teachers; that didn't happen often. I tried unsuccessfully to shake off my depression. Life was sometimes fantastic and sometimes mediocre, ordinary, and often boring. I knew this but was still depressed. I hid my depression by acting out and experimenting with alcohol. I was disgusted with myself for drinking; I didn't want to be like my dad.

Alcoholism may be genetic but it is also a learnt behaviour. Although I only lived with dad until I was six, this is the time when our personalities are shaped, and we are greatly influenced by our environment. I suppose I craved the release alcohol gave me from the stress in my life, and I enjoyed pretending the world was a happier place than I knew it to be.

Reportedly, if one of your parents is an alcoholic, the chance of becoming one yourself increases by fifty percent, which is pretty huge. I wasn't really worried about becoming an alcoholic, but I sure felt messed up. I had a great social life and good friends with whom I could talk about most of my issues, but I couldn't talk about my background.

I never wagged school or missed classes; school gave me a sense of belonging, even if I didn't excel at it. I had no ambitions to go to university or be anyone of any great significance. Basically, if I could cope with my day-to-day routine, I thought I was doing okay. Handing in homework was a part of that. Working part-time, doing my homework, and seeing whomever I was going out with on the weekends was all I did. That was all I could cope with on top of the simmering emotions from my early childhood.

Not surprisingly, I thought about suicide a lot from age fifteen to seventeen. Often I dreamt about ways of doing myself in. Nobody knew how depressed I could get, as my true feelings were buried under my mucking-around clown act. More than once I would try to see how much alcohol I could drink in one session. Maybe I was trying to numb my feelings and didn't really care if I made it through the night. Luckily for me I always vomited, which I am sure saved me a stretch or two getting my stomach pumped in hospital.

Another plan was to swerve in front of an oncoming truck during my morning bike ride to high school. The road was very busy at that time of day with many trucks, buses, and cars doing seventy kilometres per hour. Rowen, Sharon, and I rode as near to the gutter as we could for safety as we shared the road with the traffic. Often the trucks would go flying past, knocking us around with their turbulence. "You can do it!" I would tell myself as I sized up a huge truck about to pass, "Just do it quickly and it'll be all over." But I never did. I didn't really want to die, I just wanted to stop feeling so depressed.

Although I did know it as a teenager, my depression was a result of my childhood. Children of alcoholics are at greater risk of having emotional problems, including anxiety, obsessive-compulsive disorder, depression, hoarding, and phobias. Their health care costs are thirty-two percent higher. Seventy percent of children of alcoholics develop a pattern of addictive behaviour as adults, including alcoholism, overeating, and drug abuse. Many have suffered from some form of neglect, witnessed domestic violence, or have been abused physically, mentally, emotionally, and spiritually.

I found some wonderful information at www.addictioninfamily.com that I paraphrase here.

> Sadly it's not just the abuse children of alcoholics have to put up with, it's the lingering emotional chaos that permeates their life, of which I am a classic example. For example, they see themselves as perpetual victims, feeling powerless over their life circumstances, and feeling hopeless.
>
> When I was a teenager, I was a people pleaser. To avoid rejection or abandonment, I did almost anything to hang on to my relationships with my boyfriends because they appeared to care for me, no matter how bad or abusive the relationship. I was too loyal for my own good, even when I knew that they didn't deserve my loyalty.
>
> Seeking approval is also something these children do, just as I did. I went to almost any lengths to win the love and approval from my boyfriends which I desperately longed for. I felt as if I never got the support that I needed from the people that mattered most to me when I was growing up
>
> Other common behaviours of children of alcoholics are fear of abandonment and a belief that they are unworthy of love, and therefore unlovable. They are extremely afraid that once someone finds out "who they really are"

they will once again be rejected and abandoned, left all alone in a cold, harsh world.

Unfortunately, children of alcoholics tend to do and become what was done to and modelled for them. Most wind up continuing the cycle of alcoholism and family dysfunction in lives. They avoid talking about or expressing their feelings, especially those related to traumatic childhood experiences—just as I did. They are often emotionally crippled, unable to feel or express feelings because of their frighteningly painful and overwhelming nature. They often have difficulty with intimacy because intimacy requires openness and vulnerability. As children, when they were open or vulnerable, they were told that they weren't up to standard and were rejected for being who they are and what they felt.

Possibly this was another basic survival skill they learnt when growing up: the need to hide their true feelings and not express them in order to protect themselves from being hurt. Sometimes, under very emotional circumstances, I still have the need to protect myself. So I act the clown, am sarcastic, and not serious, when underneath it all I'm a scared piece of jelly wobbling on my plate. I am frightened that I will fall off and splatter on the ground. Many children of alcoholics lack spontaneity, playfulness, and joy—especially when they are stressed or worried.

Other symptoms are critical self appraisal, as the children can recite long lists of what's wrong with them, yet struggle to find one positive thing to say about themselves. This was due to rarely receiving positive praise, so all they know is how to be critical of themselves. Unfortunately I still struggle with this; though I am a lot better at telling myself I have done a good job. Depression, anxiety, and stress are often a part of their lives and they suffer from higher rates of stress related diseases, mood disorders, anxiety disorders, and other serious psychopathology. Feelings of guilt and shame, low self-worth and self-esteem are issues often felt by these children and they often feel very uncomfortable with and guilty standing up for themselves and their rights –especially with family members. It's much easier for them to give in to the demands of others and carry the burden of shame and guilt for all the problems. The low self-worth and self-esteem comes from them rarely if ever getting to see them reflected back in a positive light. Generally as the child, no matter how hard he or she tried, seemed to fall short of perfection in the parents' eyes and, as such, seem to fall short of perfection in the child's own eyes. Other issues are they are control freaks, have a heightened sense of responsibility and are often caretakers.

When I was fifteen, mum and step dad decided to part ways; they had only been living a shell of a married life for many years. Nobody was upset when he left, and I never understood why they got married at all. The only good thing to come of the marriage was my younger sister, Kimberley, whom I loved with the utmost devotion and used to treat as though she was my own baby.

After my step dad left, mum and my older brother Rowen were cleaning out his darkroom and came upon a stash of "gay" books. They were pissing themselves with laughter that step dad was either gay or bisexual all this time. Mum swore she never knew, even after eight years of marriage. It was fine with us, but we were fascinated with thought of him living a lie for so long. It also threw light on a relationship he had with another man that had us a bit perplexed. It all seemed to make sense after we found those books.

I have no qualms about gay or bisexual people; I just don't understand how step dad could live a lie all those years. It seemed so sad that he couldn't admit who he really was. Eventually he remarried, but died young of a heart attack within a couple of years. As I didn't have much to do with him, I wasn't sad that he had passed, just that he appeared to have only half a life. Perhaps he found some happiness.

Chapter 3

Beginning Anew

At the end of year eleven, now seventeen, I left school and worked as a veterinary nurse in a local clinic for four years, saving all I could for a trip through Asia and the United Kingdom. I was enthusiastic and loved caring for all the animals, for whom I developed a great affinity. I had found my niche: nursing animals back from the brink.

The trust the animals placed in me made me try much harder to save them. I was such a softie and often cried with the owners when their pets passed away. Working at the vets gave me a reason to get up in the morning and it was far superior to staying at school.

My depression began to lift (even if I awoke to depression, I soon shook it off) and learnt to control my anger. Life was enjoyable, and I finally began to feel like an adult. I was still living at home with mum, Adam, and Kimberly, but Rowen had joined the army and Sharon was living with her boyfriend. So life was pretty good. After a couple of years, I grew restless. Restlessness drove me to save more so I could go overseas and, perhaps, find myself. At twenty-one, I decided to go, and told my boyfriend I was going, "With or without you."

I had a magnificent time, travelling through forty countries in twenty months, including working for a while in London. I visited Nepal, India, Pakistan, Turkey, the Middle East, the UK, Ireland, Scotland, Spain, and fourteen African countries, before finally running out of money in Cape Town.

My odyssey was one of the most rewarding and challenging times of my life, and it left me with a lifetime's worth of memories: riding a rickshaw through the streets of Delhi, visiting the Taj Mahal in Agra; rising at to watch lions strolling through the scrub in Zimbabwe; backpacking alone from Kenya to South

Africa; meeting mostly friendly locals who enriched my view of the world, often pinching myself to ensure it wasn't a dream.

One particular memory stands out. I hitched a ride through Zambia on a truck. I had my usual tins of beef and creamed corn which I liked to have together. I didn't carry cooking utensils and these didn't require heating.

We drove slowly through a little village where the children had no clothes. It reminded me of the World Vision commercials where the kids have swollen stomachs, their big eyes peering cautiously out of thin faces. A mum was putting her hand to her mouth, the universal gesture asking for food, imploring me with her eyes, so I gave her my tins of beef and corn. I didn't have anything else and went without dinner. I often wonder how those children fared—did they make it?

What a fantastic country South Africa is! I had the pleasure of really living there, and thought it very similar to Australia, including the people. They share my sense of humour, which was a treat. I would love to take our family there on holiday.

After three months working in Cape Town, I dusted off my backpack and hitch-hiked through Botswana to Victoria Falls in Zimbabwe. I hitched 1,400 kilometres and spent the first night in Johannesburg enjoying the hospitality of a wonderful local family. On the way to Maun, Botswana, I was stupid enough to climb into a very large cage with a full-grown, half-tamed cheetah. Thank God, I was with a guy who had a big chunk of meat, and he threw it at the cheetah when it charged. I remember thinking the situation would be more controlled, but I lived to tell the tale. Met some wonderful South African guys in Maun and travelled with them to Victoria Falls.

A scorpion stung me in a camp shower facility in the Chobe National Park in Botswana, 100 kilometres from civilization. It was dark, and my torch wasn't working. While I showered, the scorpion curled up in my towel, and stung me when I started to dry off. I couldn't see it, but decided it must have been a scorpion—too small for a snake.

The fact that I was stung on my middle finger and nowhere else was a blessing; imagine being stung on the bum or somewhere else—ouch! That night I curled up in my sleeping bag, cuddling my backpack. I must have been fairly out of it; I didn't do any first aid procedure like wrap my finger, hand, and arm. I basically crawled into my tent and fell asleep. Thinking about it later, I realized I was extremely stupid not to take the situation more seriously.

Realistically I knew the Savuti Desert, which is situated in Chobe National Park, had no lodges to speak of in 1989. It was a desert with scorching sun and burning sand during the day. Maun was the closest town, and we'd have to drive for hours along a four wheel drive track before we found the main highway to Maun. From there, it would be another couple of hours to reach Maun.

Maun wasn't a major town, but might have had a doctor, who I might have found in the middle of the night, and who might have anti-venom. I didn't really know what had bitten me, and I didn't like my chances of going to all that effort without finding help. I'd read somewhere that if you stayed still and didn't get excited, the venom would move slowly enough for your lymph to eliminate it and that's what I decided to do.

I passed out very quickly but woke a couple of hours later to a hyena squeezing past my tent, nearly collapsing it. He was attracted to the remains of our dinner. African spotted hyenas average about fifty kilogrammes, with the female being slightly larger, but can weigh up to seventy kilogrammes. They're eighty-to-ninety centimetres at the shoulder, strongly built, and have powerful, bone-crushing jaws.

Hyenas are usually considered scavengers, but they are also effective predators. The thought that one of them was only inches away, with only the thin fabric of the tent separating us, startled the shit out of me. I began to realise that I hadn't gone to hell, but was actually still alive. I sat there, bolt upright, wondering how to defend myself. To my relief, the hyena found another way to pass back through our campsite and didn't again come near my tent. We headed out the next day, but I passed out intermittently for the next twenty-four hours.

The local animals seem to have had it in for me. Earlier that day we'd been away from camp for a few hours. When we returned, I noticed my tent was open and had been ransacked. The guys I was with said it was undoubtedly a baboon, who are highly intelligent. Not only had he ransacked my clothes and pulled everything I owned out of my backpack, it had sucked the red sugar colouring off my pain killers. I found half-chewed pills all over my tent. Maybe the baboon had a headache?

After leaving the park, we travelled to Victoria Falls and then to Harare where the South African guys introduced me to a fantastic group of people. I spent three incredible months with these new friends. My time in Africa, developing survival skills, talking to locals, learning to live on my own, gaining independence, all helped shape the person I am today.

Travelling through Africa was amazing, but I discovered that no amount of pretence will fool yourself. My depression, resentment, anger, fear, sadness, and feelings of failure emerged when I got home. Although there were a few snags, I had spent a mostly fabulous time overseas. Travelling, meeting interesting people, and experiencing amazing cultures were all great, but the best part being overseas is that no one knew me. I could escape from being an alcoholic's daughter and pretend that life was one big party with no hassles or obligations.

In spite of the magnificent time I had travelling—even learning to stick up for myself against machine-gun wielding border guards—I couldn't shake the feeling that there was something fundamentally wrong with me. Coming home, it seemed to others that I had changed; I was more assertive and stronger mentally. Inside, I was crumbling, and I had to admit my problems. Everything inside me was messed up, and my tightly held emotions were starting to crack. For too long I had tried to suppress my emotions; I was about to erupt.

Then I stumbled across a brilliant book that led me to Al-Anon. Al-Anon is a fellowship that provides support and comfort for anyone who's been affected by another's problem drinking. At the meetings I learnt about the illness of alcoholism and tried to understand how dad's drinking affected our family. I was free to express what I really thought within secure walls.

It was a long time coming and very hard to communicate my true feelings over the wall I had built around me. Al-Anon helped me realise there are other children, spouses, and friends of alcoholics who were trying to survive, just as I was. We seemed to have a lot in common: many of us have low self-esteem and little self-worth. Coming to terms with our past and refusing to allow it to take control of our present or future is a long and painful process.

Seeking help in Al-Anon was the first step to recovery, and discovering just who the hell I was. Sharing my experiences and hearing others (many even more harrowing) made me stronger. The uncritical, non-judgemental approach emphasized taking control of one's life and learning to act rather than react, helped me to cope and accept my reality. This helped me to face life in a more understanding and positive way, rather than as a victim.

The best lesson I learned at Al-Anon was to control my anger and stop directing it at people whom I loved. I learnt to tell the people who had pissed me off what was bothering me, rather than allowing my anger to build until it exploded at one of my friends. I didn't like confronting people, especially when I didn't like what they were doing, yet I slowly learnt to let them know what I thought more subtly and without anger.

The funny thing—in an ironic way—was learning how strong I am. My upbringing, even with all its negatives, had a positive side: because it made me an incredibly strong person and gave me massive endurance.

I grew strong enough mentally and physically to travel overseas including a year backpacking through Africa and spending seven months in a tent with no hot shower, even encountering and surviving moments of terror.

While writing this book, which was to be only about my daughter Avelynn and her strength coping with chronic illnesses, a friend asked, "Michelle, where do you get the strength to cope with Avelynn and all her problems? How do you manage so well when she's in hospital and your husband's away?" Even a few of the nurses commented on how well I dealt with Avelynn and shook their heads in amazement.

I know where my strength comes from; it was not something I need to think about. Coping was a skill as ingrained as talking. It's become second nature for me to go on with it and not complain, just put my head down and get on with it. It never occurred to me that I was stronger than most when it came to stressful situations.

I don't usually want to divulge my back ground, I just say something like, "Yeah, I had a bit of a rough upbringing. Dad was an alcoholic." But I rarely talk about it because I don't usually have time to explain and it's unpleasant to discuss. Plus there's rarely time to talk about the benefit: it made me stronger. Most people don't really understand. For six months, I stopped writing search my soul. I really wasn't sure what to write or what was relevant. But, I thought, maybe I can actually help someone who reads this book.

Many people have told me I am such a strong person to cope with all the turmoil my family has been through, especially with my husband in the in the army and later working in Iraq.

I nearly stopped writing all together because I am not comfortable sharing my story. After analysing my upbringing, I knew I couldn't avoid answering those questions, or not write this book. Of course, my upbringing and subsequent travels through Asia, Europe, and Africa made me the person I am today.

Avelynn, my youngest daughter, opened the door to a deeper understanding of the strength I have. If it weren't for Avelynn, I wouldn't have really understood my own strength. Initially, I wasn't going to mention my background but focus on Avelynn—her strength and inspiration. What finally prompted me, after much time and deliberation, to share my experiences and bare my attempts to establish control over my life was the possibility that I could help someone else gain insight into how to take mastery of his or her life.

After reading about suicide and depression rates amongst teenagers and adults in Australia and other western countries, I thought if I could stop someone from going down that road by baring my soul, it would be worthwhile. We never know what's around the corner. Throughout my life, I have never given up hope; even now, when I don't know how much longer Avelynn will live, I don't give up hope.

Variations on my story have been played over and over again by many people; it is not that exceptional. Many families are touched by alcoholism, abuse, and other factors leading to depression and self-harm. On a positive note, a lot of the great leaders of the world have come from broken homes or are orphans. To overcome obstacles and reach for the sky, you have to be tough.

Alcoholism is rife in Australia: suicide rates are too high, and depression remains a serious problem. As a society, we must help depressed teenagers. Once I found out these statistics I couldn't live with myself without bringing this information to light. Yet another reason I wrote this book, for we all have a great desire to be loved and appreciated for ourselves—we are all truly valuable.

Are you ready for some facts?

Around 2,000 Aussies commit suicide every year, more than are killed on the road. I would like to know what we're doing about it. Suicide accounts for nearly twenty percent of all deaths amongst young men aged twenty to thirty-four. Though successful suicide rates for teenagers are quite low, a nearly unbelievable one-in-twelve teenagers attempt suicide. About one-in-five teenagers suffers from depression before they reach the age of eighteen. The rate of depression among teenagers is unacceptably high: nearly twice as high as in the general adult population.

Between twenty and fifty percent of teens who suffer from depression have a family history of depression or other mental conditions. Nearly thirty percent abuse drugs, alcohol, or other chemicals. Severe, untreated depression often results in suicide and nearly ninety percent of suicides suffered from depression or other mental conditions. Sadly, only one-third of depressed teenagers get professional help and even fewer complete treatment. However, eight out of ten who attempt suicide had sought some kind of help.

To catch depression early, it's extremely important for parents, caregivers, and friends to watch for these signs of depression in boys and girls ages of nine and older:

- Lack of interest in attending school and constantly finding excuses to be absent
- Loss of enthusiasm to do things that normally get them excited
- Declining communication with siblings, friends, and family
- Trouble eating or sleeping
- Constantly feeling sad, down, or depressed
- Crying for no apparent reason
- Lack of concentration, lack of focus, memory loss, bad grades

If you want to know more, please search the Internet for "depression in teenagers" or seek professional advice. There's so much fantastic information available, but I wanted to highlight the issue in this book, especially after personally suffering the debilitating effects of depression.

Like everyone, I wanted to be accepted and valued for who I was and to know I was truly loved and appreciated. But I never experienced that acceptance or love as a child. Dad's emotional abuse was so intense, and so hurtful that I felt unlovable. Although I knew mum loved me, and she showed me love in many ways. However, my dad's violence took centre stage. Because he was so hurtful, I withered under from his onslaughts. I had to protect myself or I would have died.

Studies show that depressed girls are often too embarrassed to discuss their problems, whatever they may be:. A family history of depression, stress at home, bad grades, peer pressure, obesity, body image, fear of abandonment, illness, disability, and the stress of coping with hormonal and other physiological change all contribute to depression.

Always remember, you are loved, you are special, and there's no one in the world like you. Understand that we all have different values and each see the world in our unique way. It's not right or wrong, just different, according to what's most important to us. Don't try to become someone you're not, or to conform to someone else's idea of what is good for you. You have unique talents and can have an inspired and purposeful life.

The most significant knowledge I have gained is from Dr. John Demartini, a human behavioural specialist. He taught me that there can't be a positive without a negative. Because of our values and perceptions, we usually choose to see only one side at a time. I have done an enormous amount of work and I know that every time dad abused me emotionally or physically, my mum, sister, brother, or my beloved cat was with me.

My daughter Avelynn is chronically ill, but our entire family has learnt valuable lessons from seeing her cope with life. She doesn't feel sorry for herself. My perception basically deceived me into believing that only a bad thing was happening. Now I know that in every adversity, and in every challenge, there lies a reward. Go look for it!

Chapter 4

Michelle & Peter Finally Meet:

With the help of Al-Anon, I recognised certain character traits in myself that weren't beneficial. For example, my inappropriate anger, which I usually directed at the wrong person. Or, my addiction to the downs and ups in my life because that was how I was raised. More importantly, I learnt that the guys I had been attracted to were "charmers" or the ones I thought I could change, even whilst accepting their criticism of me and putting up with other negative traits.

I learnt that I had to empower myself; that I was lovable. I didn't have to put up with crap, and most of all I was worth taking care of. The guys I was attracted to were bad boys or the non-committed ones that I knew I could never marry. Going to Al-Anon dramatically changed my perspective. I learnt to respect myself, and I didn't have to change who I was. If I met someone who didn't like me or who tried to change who I was, then they weren't right for me. I opened myself up to meeting a nicer guy, not one who was a charmer or treated me like shit.

Life can be ironic. One of our three flatmates in the house in Glen Waverley moved out about two weeks after I arrived. We placed an advert in the local paper that was answered by Peter Wood, who is now my husband. Proof that the universe does listen—sometimes anyway!

I opened the door and there stood Peter and his mate, who was drop-dead gorgeous, but too young for me. That was it. Peter said he took one look at me and knew he wanted to marry me. He says it was my sexy legs, which I was proud to say looked pretty good as I ran five kilometres a few times a week. I didn't need much convincing to go out with him either—he also had sexy legs.

Actually he had a cute arse, which is always a winner for me and very nice, intense blue eyes. Within two weeks we were going out, but somehow managed to keep it a secret from our flatmates. We didn't want it to be awkward if we broke up and we didn't want to be uncomfortable around them. Looking back I don't know why we cared so much; I suppose a secret romance was more exciting. We felt like teenagers, although Peter was approaching thirty and I was twenty-six. We would jump apart when one of the other guys came home when we were watching TV together. This was rather funny sometimes.

For a laugh, I'll tell you about Peter's drop-dead gorgeous mate. He's better looking than Hugh Grant or any other movie star. I often couldn't speak properly around him as "the cat got my tongue." Occasionally I'd think I had the house to myself coming back from a run, covered in sweat, hair in a mess, my face bright red. I'd open the front door, often talking to myself, when suddenly I'd hear laughter coming from the lounge room. In I'd go, turn ever redder seeing Peter and his mate, and promptly leave. I finally got used to him, and he ceased to have that effect on me. Ever been in that situation?

I'd like to tell you it was all smooth sailing from there, but I would be lying; it was that far from the truth. I was still trying to sort out my shit, so to speak, through Al-Anon. Peter had just arrived from James Cook University in the hot tropics of Queensland, and he was having a wee bit of culture shock in nontropical Melbourne. He was just getting started at his new university at Monash, while settling into our house. He was trying to rejoin the army reserve commando unit in Williamstown.

Both of us had a lot of reshuffling to do, as well as trying to have a secret romance. In March 2003, Peter had just turned thirty, and was considering a career change. He was studying economics, politics, and the Indonesian language at Monash in preparation for applying to the Department of Foreign Affairs in Canberra. Peter spoke only briefly of his time in the SASR and never mentioned rejoining his old regiment. I was working at a local vet's enjoying being with the animals that I loved.

My Little Red Head

Chapter 5

Peter's Story

I was nineteen when I joined the Australian Army in April 1981, to be a rifleman and paratrooper. I had seen enough war films to think parachuting was cool. After six months of training, I was posted as a rifleman to the 5/7th battalion Royal Australian Regiment which was a mechanised infantry battalion. "Mechanised" just meant we usually travelled in armoured personnel carriers rather than on foot.

When I joined, the Australian Army was reorganizing its paratroopers. Becoming a paratrooper meant waiting for years and obtaining a battalion transfer. I realised while I was with 5/7 RAR in Sydney that there was another parachute unit that I could join: the elite 1st Special Air Service Regiment (SASR). I quickly learned that this unit had one of the most arduous and rigorous selection processes in the world. I was contemptuously told that I would not pass the selection process.

All I wanted to be was a rifleman and jump out of perfectly good aeroplane on the end of a parachute. Despite much ridicule and some encouragement, I started to train and prepare for the SAS selection course almost two years away. I was too young and inexperienced to consider an SAS selection course any sooner.

In early June 1983 I arrived, a bit fearful and concerned, at the training centre for the Royal Australian Infantry Corps (near Singleton in NSW) to attend the SAS selection course. This three-week "cadre course" was the main component of the twelve-month SAS selection process.

In the previous two years, I had become quite an athlete and was particularly good at forced marching with a heavy pack. My personal training regimen had focused on ten kilometre runs carrying a 4.7 kg self-loading rifle and accessories, as well as thirty-kilometre marches wearing a thirty-kilogramme pack. I was reasonably confident with my fitness level, but was I good enough the pass the unknown elements of the cadre course?

To my horror, I discovered that physical fitness only accounted for about ten percent of the cadre course, and the other ninety percent measured mental toughness. The first five days were designed to wear down physical strength and show the applicants where their pain barriers were and how far they could be pushed.

The pain barrier was all about mental toughness. I realised that the SAS ideal was being able to perform and complete your mission when all other soldiers had lost the will. The rest of the course was sheer willpower as the steadily diminishing number of survivors became more and more physically exhausted. The amazing thing about the cadre course is that all applicants are volunteers. They can quit the course at any time rather than completing the selection process.

What motivated me to continue with this seriously painful course? I initially only wanted to jump from perfectly good aircraft. I discovered the answer in a demon called the "fear of failure." It's a powerful motivator that can push someone through surprisingly difficult situations. The fear of failure, and the peer pressure not to disappoint your mates, are the strongest motivators for surviving and passing the cadre course.

One example of mental toughness was a mate we called Whitey, who was hospitalised after our selection because his feet were stripped of their skin during our long runs and marches in heavy boots.

The "cut-away drill" was another toughener. When the main parachute fails to open, the cut-away drill uses a release ripcord to cut away the main 'chute and allow the reserve 'chute to open. During a "fun" phase of the course that included forced marches day and night without sleep, we were given a short bus ride to the bottom of a hill. The bus stopped, and we were told to get out and move as individuals with our heavy packs and rifles to the top of the hill, where we would be given our next instructions.

The candidates were ever given only minimal information, and never knew what was next. Managing the resulting stress was part of the selection process. As we got off the bus, we sensed that we needed to get to the top of the hill as quickly as possible; this appeared to be a timed event. That damned hill was obviously picked because it was a series of false crests and seemed to go on forever as we trudged up a four-wheel-drive track with our packs and rifles.

At the top, the one the directing staff (DS) for the course was recording our names and times and then assigning our next task. The DS told me, "Well done, Ranger Wood, that was a good time. Now your next task is a quick lunch followed by another happy wander through these small hills." That section of the course was called The Happy Wanderer, after the SASR regimental parade quick march tune.

My personal version of the cut-away drill followed. I was so exhausted that I crapped my pants while the DS was briefing me. I had to do the penguin walk over to some bushes and cut away my underpants with a knife before I flopped on the ground. I was so stuffed at that stage I lacked the strength to hold my sphincter shut. After a quick lunch I headed to the next check point and a briefing on the next task.

I passed the SAS selection and thoroughly enjoyed the next eight years before exhaustion and the intense training wore me down. After a year studying at James Cook University, I transferred to Monash University in Melbourne. Answering the "flatmate wanted" advert in the local paper was the best; I was thrilled to meet my new flatmate (and future wife) Michelle.

My Little Red Head

Chapter 6

Welcome to the Army, Perth, & Marriage

Over the Easter holiday 2003, I went home for a few days without Peter (he was off in the bush somewhere on a Reserve week) and I realized that I missed him. My mum said she knew I was serious about Peter as it was the first guy I said I missed. "Oh shit!" I thought. She was right, but I was scared of making a commitment. Both of us had been thinking of getting hitched, but were too scared to even mention it.

One sunny day, at the start of a five kilometre run, Peter casually mentioned that he was rejoining his old SAS regiment. I said, "Okay, where does that leave us?" "Well I thought that maybe you could come," said Peter. "Yeah. Well, I'm not quitting my job and moving 3,500 kilometres to Perth for no reason." "Yeah. Well, um, I suppose we'd better make it a bit more permanent." Peter said in typical military style. "So ya mean like, we'd be together on a permanent basis. Like, get engaged first, that kind of thing?" I asked. "Yes, well…okay." Peter said.

Without any ado, we ran five kilometres and chatted about our engagement. Ironically, Peter never asked, "Will you marry me?" But we both knew we were talking about getting hitched, getting married! By November, we were engaged and our romance no longer secret.

Little did we know that we were already a family. We could not have cared less what people thought, but it was very fast. Peter had expressed how serious we were about having kids, "Well if you're not pregnant now, you soon will be." We were no longer spring chickens.

Peter finishing his Bachelor of Arts at Monash in Melbourne, and we had a couple of months before he rejoined the SAS Regiment Army in Perth. I was finally with the one bloke I didn't want to lose, so I quit my job at the vets and said good-bye to our crazy New Zealand flatmates. Typically, I didn't give the flies a chance to stick; we met, got pregnant, moved to Perth and got married in thirteen months. Best thing I ever did!

Peter and I never really went through "the wanting a baby thing" as I called it. We never discussed when to have a baby, we just knew what we wanted, and wham, I was pregnant. My body told me as soon as I met Peter, "He's the one, go for it!" We wanted at least two or three children and agreed they should be a couple of years apart. My mum had Rowen, Sharon, and me within twenty-six months, and I found that daunting. "No way—that's not for me." I thought.

Both of us had pets growing up, and I naively thought, "I've nurtured animals, how much trouble could a baby be?" Leaving mum, my baby expert, behind in Melbourne didn't bother me; I truly believed that I would be fine.

In March 2004, I was five months pregnant, and the Army were ready for Peter to rejoin his regiment. Off we went, driving my little four-cylinder, eighteen-year-old Toyota 3,500 kilometres across Australia from Melbourne to Perth. My car did exceedingly well, although we never drove faster than ninety kilometres per hour.

Crossing the Nullarbor plain is an amazing trek and is one of Australia's greatest road journeys. At its widest, the Nullarbor stretches about 1,100 kilometres; its apt name is derived from the Latin for "no trees." The Eyre Highway is the only road across the Nullarbor, but it is paved. Signs show the distance to the next town with petrol and other services. Its name honours explorer Edward John Eyre, who in 1841 barely survived thirst, hunger, and treacherous guides to make the first east-west crossing of the continent. The Eyre Highway crosses only a small section of treeless plain; most of the remainder is flat, arid or semiarid, and almost treeless.

"Fabulous—this should be fun!" I thought, remembering a car and caravan trip across the Nullarbor when I was nine. I had forgotten how much the heat would affect me when I was pregnant. It was the end of summer, hottest time of year. With no air conditioning and temperatures above forty degrees Celsius. I was an uncomfortable, whinging, complaining, and pregnant elephant. "I'm so sorry Peter," I'd say, pouring another litre of water over my head in an attempt to cool down while he was driving. Trying my best not to cry from the intense heat, I improvised sun shields, which I had to move every time the sun changed direction.

Afternoons were the worst; the sun would pour directly on us through the windscreen. I used wet towels, newspapers, whatever we had, and tried my best to attach them to the windscreen without blocking Peter's view. But to no avail: it was just hot! We'd gotten only to Adelaide (about 700 kilometres) when Peter announced he'd had enough, was at his wits end, and would put me on a plane over to Perth.

But the clouds miraculously rolled in, and it rained lightly all the way to Perth. It was the first time I was overjoyed to see rain. I am a sun worshipper; I love to sunbathe and I live for hot weather. Not this time—I was rapturous over the cooler weather, thinking, "Thank you, thank you, thank you, wonderful rain!"

I eagerly anticipated our arrival in Perth and our marriage ceremony. The was in the local registry office with only two of Peter's cousins—strangers to me—as witnesses. Peter and I thought becoming engaged was a bigger affair and wanted to be married without fanfare. We booked the Registry Office in Perth before we left Melbourne. I have an adventurous spirit and was confident all would be well—what could go wrong?

Arriving in Perth, I was a bit dismayed at the burnt grass and what appeared to be sand in people's gardens. If you dug to plant a tree, it was all sand. I was fascinated by the contrast to Melbourne, where there is real dirt that turns to thick mud. I already missed the green of Melbourne and Victoria. Perth only receives rain five or six months per year, and it hadn't rained for months.

A lot of people used bore-water for their gardens because the alternative was a patch of brown grass amongst the sand patches. The good thing was our lawn only required mowing three or four times a year. Grass just didn't grow, even with bore-water and fertilizer. In Melbourne, we try to kill off the lawn because it grew too quickly, and you'd spend nearly every weekend mowing it down. Now I was in Perth, where people spent a lot of money trying to grow grass—weird.

It was stinking hot, close to forty degrees Celsius during the day, and Brett's house (where we stayed) didn't have an electric fan, much less an air conditioner. It was close to thirty degrees Celsius the night we arrived. It was difficult to sleep. With the heat and the move, I got pissed off again.

On our way across the Nullarbor, Peter had told me about the local market in Hay Street. There are some great local craft markets in Melbourne, and I loved shopping around them and I was keen to compare the crafts and the local goods in Perth. So I woke early the next day, eager to visit the local market in Hay Street.

After a shower and getting dressed, I started brushing my long, knotty hair. I flicked my hair to one side, as always, but I flicked too hard, or my neck was still stiff from our trip, or my hormones were off, who knows? I screamed in pain, fell to the floor, and blacked-out. After a few minutes, I came-to and managed to crawl down the hall way to the bedroom, calling Peter to come rescue me.

The pain was excruciating; Peter and his best friend couldn't move or even touch me. When tried to lift my head, I passed out again. The Australian ambulance service is fantastic, and the four guys put me on a stretcher. Brett, who was Peter's best friend, must have thought me a total loser.

Peter wondered whom he was marrying; if I gave myself whiplash whilst brushing my hair, what else was I capable of? Yes, very funny. Ha, ha, ha, what a dick-head! For the next two weeks, I sat on the couch in a neck brace, complained about the heat, and counted the hours until my next pain-killer. Welcome to Perth!

After that incident, Brett didn't think much of me and decided to take quarters on the base as soon as possible. It took quite a while to convince him that I didn't do it on purpose, but Peter and I bought nearly all of his furniture and took over his place on a permanent basis. We were only twenty minutes drive from the barracks, where Peter was welcomed back into the army life. My neck continued to be a source of great amusement for the Army guys and their wives whom I met while still wearing my brace, but I was welcomed. Don't ya just love it!

Peter wasn't in a typical regiment; this was the Special Air Service. The SASR is Australia's pride and joy, an elite regiment of about 700, with just 300 fighters, divided into Sabre Squadrons. Each squadron has a support team of fifty or so. The support teams are called Black Hats amongst the guys in Perth and are part of the regular Army. The support staff include cooks and clerks, as well as guys and girls that work in the Q-store ("Queesʺ) just to name a few.

The distinction between fighters and support staff can create a gulf between their spouses. The fighters are "beret qualified." Often another army wife would ask if my husband was beret qualified. If I answered, "Yes," she wouldn't talk to me, which I found unbelievable. I learnt to say, "Yes my husband is in the Army. My name's Michelle and I am pleased to meet you," ignoring the question. I wasn't into the whole hierarchy of it all. Some of the wives lived through their husbands, but most didn't— including me. I made lots of friends whose husbands were either in the Army or not, black hat or beret qualified; it didn't matter to me as long as we got along.

On the 21 March 1994, Peter and I tied the knot at the Registry Office in front of our witnesses; Peter's cousins whom I had just met the previous night. The most memorable moment was Peter trying to squeeze our little car into the smallest space in the Registry building car park and side-swiping a concrete pole. I wasn't that nervous, but I think Peter was. I just wanted it over. How sweet that my tough SAS guy was more nervous about tying the knot than I was. Peter's beloved grandmother, "Nana Win" as I called her, was so excited about her favourite grandson getting married (and I really didn't think it mattered to whom) that she managed to get into every bloody photo.

Picture this: it's forty-two degrees Celsius and I'm five months pregnant. After our wedding, we're in one of Perth's gardens without any shade. I wanted us to hurry up, get a decent photo, and get the hell into some air-conditioning before I passed away. Peter's cousins are camera crazy and took so many photos that my eyes watered from the flashes and bright sun. "Nana Win" positioned herself in every photo, even after I explained that we had enough photos of her.

This went on and on until I finally cracked and announced the pregnant lady had enough and was going to pass out if she didn't get into air-conditioning, pronto! I didn't have romantic ideas about getting married and neither did Peter, so I wore a white top and black pants, which were the only ones that fitted me. I might have worn a dress if I had found one, but the summer fashion season was over. After sweltering all day in those black pants, I chucked them in the bin.

Peter's family realised how incredibly hot I was and made amends by keeping me supplied with iced drinks when we returned home. I wasn't pissed off all day, but it wasn't the most enjoyable experience I ever had. However, we had a great time that night at a local Chinese restaurant.

Chapter 7

A High-Needs Baby

Our beautiful baby girl, Ayla, was born that August, a week later than expected. At nearly nine pounds, about four kilogrammes, she was a big bouncing baby and broke my coccyx. "Come on, Michelle, you can turn around and see your baby!" The midwife said. "No, I bloody well can't; I'm in so much pain, I can't move," I replied.

I didn't believe in pain killers for birth (yes, I am one of those weirdos). I had insisted in going to a birthing centre attached to the main maternity hospital, King Edward, locally known as "Kind Edward." Once I'd broken my coccyx (tailbone) I was screaming for pain relief, my bum hurt sooooo much. This wasn't a great introduction to parenthood for me, and neither was Ayla, who screamed black and blue with colic for six weeks, the longest weeks of our lives. "Oh! You've got one of those babies," the health care nurse said, "You just have to hang in there and handle it the best you can" That was her best advice. "What the dickens, can't anyone help me?" I thought to myself.

The best advice I took was from a fantastic lactation consultant who said "You've got a high need baby, one that needs to be attached to you," and taught me how to wear Ayla in a sling and breast feed her properly. The sling worked like a charm, and Ayla remained literally attached to me for another nine months. Wasn't I the lucky one?

I am not being mean, but a couple of hours after Ayla was born I was wondering just what the hell I had done to get such a demanding baby. Demanding isn't quite the right word. Maybe challenging, hard, tough, difficult, determined, and strong might sum up her personality. Upon meeting her at three days, the health care nurse, who came out to measure Ayla and see if

I was okay, said she'd never met a more determined child in her entire life.

Two months after Ayla's birth, the Army Married Quarters, called "Seaward Village," was officially opened by the Honourable Kim Beazley on 28 October 1994. We were lucky to be offered one of the brand-new houses in Dune Court and watched while the houses opposite us were finished off. Brett's house, though great, didn't have the advantage of sea views, wasn't within cycling distance for Peter, and was isolated from the other Army families.

I should have realized that I was to be broken in to the typical life of an "army wife," when I (not Peter) signed the official papers to our new quarters at "The Patch," as Seaward Village became affectionately known. Peter was often away, and I got used to doing things on my own, which is the army way. As Peter would often say, "If the army had wanted me to have a wife, they would have issued me one."

Not nice, but sometimes it seemed true. The Army didn't take into account how hard it was to work around Peter's schedule. Organising social events became a nightmare as there was always a possibility of a last-minute change. I was frustrated that it became the norm to change plans, book holidays at the last minute, and miss so many events. I hate cancelling things at the last minute, but this became a way of life. The worst was Peter missing some of Ayla's milestones. Miraculously, Peter was home for lunch when Ayla took her first steps, from Peter to me—how amazing was that?

I found, on "The Life of an Army Wife" web site, a quote from someone answering a journalist's question about what it was like being an army wife.

> Women always love men in uniform but a lot just don't realise what goes with that uniform…what the realities are…I never did before…coming second to the army is something that is hard to accept when in a relationship you're supposed to be number one in the other person's

> life…with the army that can't happen…it's not just a job it's a way of life…365 days a year, 24/7…

How true that is! Not only did I marry Peter, I quit my job and moved away from my home. My friends and my mum were four and a half hours away by plane. I was trying to cope with a very demanding baby, "one of those type of babies" that many of my friends said they were glad they didn't have and took pity on me.

I had to stand on my two feet, make new friends, meet the needs of Ayla and try to cope. I no longer had a job and didn't fancy leaving Ayla to be a veterinarian nurse; Peter's pay was adequate. Though I had made a couple of good friends from the pregnancy exercise classes at Kind Edward Hospital, I often felt quite alone. My magnificent Burmese cats were a great comfort and never ceased to amaze me with their affection and companionship.

In December, we took our beautiful Burmese to a cattery and flew to Melbourne to get remarried. Our relatives let us know they were incredibly put-out that we had married in Perth. Naturally, Peter couldn't fly with me and Ayla, so I had the pleasure of coping with her on my own for the four and a half hour flight. Ayla screamed most of the way, and I was glad to land. Peter followed a few days later, and we tied-the-knot once again, witnessed by our relatives, near mum's house in a beautiful garden setting in Millgrove. We were surrounded by majestic mountain ash trees and near the Yarra river.

The Yarra Valley is a world-class, world renowned, wine region, reminiscent of Bordeaux, Burgundy, or Tuscany. It is a place of pristine beauty, where the water and the air are clean and crisp, the views spectacular, and the ambience friendly and relaxing.

It was a beautiful occasion. I wore a gorgeous ivory dress of raw silk with magnificent, hand-made lace, and Peter wore a matching ivory suit. Our bridesmaids were dressed in deep, rich burgundy, and, of course, our little sweet baby was cute in a light pink dress. We considered ourselves lucky that Ayla didn't cry throughout our ceremony and appeared to actually like some of my relatives who took turns holding her.

Our second ceremony sharply contrasted with our first, and may have struck some as strange, as it included a poem about cats, whom we love a bit too much perhaps. Other than needing assistance to take my dress practically off every hour or so to breast-feed Ayla, now four months old, and Peter's mum feeding her red jelly, our second wedding was great! The best part was catching up with my relatives and friends in Melbourne whom I hadn't seen since March.

I could have done without the fuss; I wasn't romantic and the thought of dressing up in white and going to all that bother for one day wasn't exactly my cup of tea. I enjoyed myself thoroughly, but I still thought it a waste of money. We already had our piece of paper, and no ceremony could make Peter's and my marriage more special than it already was.

Flying back to Melbourne brought back my loneliness—it seemed that so much had happened so fast. I was trying to adjust to life with my little baby, and Ayla was quickly adjusting to life outside the womb and did not scream as often.

I had taken her to an allergy specialist who put me on the strictest diet possible as Ayla was exposed to the food I ate when she breast-fed. So I ate no milk or milk products, wheat, nuts, onions, garlic, artificial colours or flavours, sauces, bread, biscuits (unless they were homemade), eggs, or alcohol. This was tough but worth it. I shrank down to fifty kilograms within four months. I felt great but was always hungry. I tried soy milk for Ayla, and she vomited; I tried lots of different things and milk substitutes, which she promptly vomited. Finally, I finally found a predigested milk formula that won the day. But Ayla was still attached to me and to breast feeding, though I supplemented with the formula.

About this time Ayla developed bladder and ear infections with such regularity that we could find our way to the doctor's even blindfolded. I was under the naive impression that babies were supposed to immediately be the highlight of your life...very wrong. Ayla fussed and was easily bothered by changes in her environment. She settled poorly at night, required an hour's rocking to sleep, and didn't accept strangers. If I put her down, she'd cry. She was not a self-soother, and wanted to nurse all the time. She was intense and acted as if she were always in high gear, waking frequently in the night. Ayla was hyperactive and hypertonic, she drained my energy and wore me out. I often worried about how long I could cope and what I could expect as she got older.

Not surprisingly, Peter could hardly manage with her when he came home from work; he'd never even held a baby before Ayla. My abilities were being stretched to breaking point. Ayla usually didn't want Peter to hold her, appearing to want only me. Ayla and I had developed a strong bond, and I was determined to be a great mum. Unfortunately, I tried to cope on my own. I couldn't give her to anyone to look after; not that anyone volunteered.

I felt it was all on me, and eventually I cracked—literately cracked. I had enough of the bullshit, the lack of support, and severe lack of sleep. I was going out of my mind with stress. After one particularly bad day, I reached my breaking point. I had spent the day crying, either by myself or whilst holding Ayla while she cried, holding her to me and trying to soothe us both by rocking and even singing a bit

Ayla was having a really bad day, and nothing I did seemed to help. I had no any relatives nearby for support, and I felt my friends didn't seem interested in holding her or giving me a break. Peter was working full-time and unable to help during the days. There was no one to help for even ten minutes to give me a break.

Most days, Ayla was with me from seven in the morning until five in the afternoon. One day, after ten hours of caring for a very demanding baby, I had fucking had it. Peter came home tired from work and laid down for a snooze. I was obviously upset.

My eyes were red from crying,. I did not have one break all day. I used to laugh when I read about mothers saying they didn't get five minutes a day to themselves. Bullshit, I had thought; but not anymore. Peter wasn't listening to me, he was just lying on the bed, about to fall asleep when I just lost it.

Instead of losing it outwardly, and giving Peter a big dose of verbal abuse, I lost it internally, which was far worse. It was like a bomb exploded in my brain and shattered my ability to think. My heart felt the unjustness of my situation. I thought Peter was a real bastard for not helping me with Ayla or listening to me. So, I left.

It was a real effort not to kick him in the crown jewels (as he calls them) as he lay stretched out on the bed. I felt like beating the shit out of him. Instead, I decided I'd had enough of him not helping me or listening to me. I wanted to leave, not hang around and argue as I had done so many times before, in a vain attempt to make him understand how very stressed I was.

I said, "Here you take care of Ayla," and walked out of the room while he was still on the bed. I grabbed my keys and handbag and drove off in our only car. I didn't know what I was going to do except, that I had to get the hell away from both of them. I had the weird idea of driving to Darwin, 4,000 kilometres north. If I followed the coast road, I thought, I would eventually find my way there, but I had no clear idea where I was going or how to get there. I didn't have a mobile phone.

Stupidly, I headed into the unknown without water, food, or a map. Perth is one of the world's most isolated cities, and once I left it, there were only scattered small towns along the way. I wasn't thinking very well, and I wanted to get the hell out of my own life. I couldn't, but that's what I wanted to do.

Have you ever been so desperate the only way you know to react is to run away? It was an incredibly unintelligent way to deal with my situation, but I was at my wits' end. Speaking to Peter didn't seem to help, and he didn't seem to be able to help. Something snapped in my head and I had to go, just get the hell away from Ayla, Peter, and my life.

I am a very tough cookie but the lack of sleep and understanding nearly killed me emotionally. I didn't think much as I followed the coast road north, hoping I'd find road signs to lead me further. My brain had tuned itself out, but I thought I could find my way without a map to Alice Springs. For some reason, I'd decided to go there.

Following the coast, it never occurred to me to turn back. I had frozen breast milk in the freezer which Ayla could have in her bottle if she so desired, and I never thought about the consequences of leaving Ayla with Peter. The fact that they didn't get along and she'd probably scream all night, never crossed my mind. I was focused solely on saving myself and my sanity.

Two hours later I arrived in Lancelin, a small fishing village and tourist town about 110 kilometres north of Perth. For the life of me, I couldn't find a way from there farther up the coast. I was dead tired, but not suicidal. I decided to stop for the night, catch some sleep, and find my way in the morning. Credit cards are great aren't they? "Who needed cash?" I thought, as I paid for my night's accommodation.

I rang up Peter that night. He was very quiet, having finally realised how far I had been pushed to end up in this position. He begged me to come home, but I was determined to keep going. I told him in no uncertain words, "You can bloody well cope with the screaming monster!" I spoke about Ayla like she was a freaking leach, sucking my life's blood out of me.

I told Peter good and proper that I couldn't continue; that I hadn't signed up to be tortured, that my life fucking sucked, that he didn't help me, that he couldn't go away and leave me anymore. On and on, I went. It was very one sided, with me doing all the yelling and Peter taking all the abuse I hurled at him. Bless him, he didn't hang up on me and promised me the world. He was extremely concerned about my sanity. Our life with this screaming, demanding baby wasn't following any of the baby books studied from cover to cover. I made no promises, but hung up on him, my heart breaking.

I didn't eat anything and tried to sleep with my boobs slowly but steadily filling with milk. I had an abundant milk, and since Ayla fed frequently, my breasts were used to being emptied at regular intervals. I got a restless night's sleep, though better than usual, and woke up around five, feeling incredibly full and sore. Though I tried my best to express some of the milk, I couldn't. Although you might think it selfish of me, that was one of the main reasons I drove back to Perth.

I decided to head home to Peter and Ayla and hoped they hadn't had a bad night. I didn't phone to let him know I was coming, as I was still feeling vindictive, disappointed, and hurtful. I kept him guessing whether or not I would come home. I wasn't sure either until I actually headed towards Perth.

I wasn't being a bitch, whatever you may think. I was in excruciating emotional pain, and felt that I had reached a crossroads and that my life was almost pointless. I felt utterly unappreciated and sick-to-death of all the well meant suggestions from friends and doctors who didn't understand why Ayla was so demanding.

Peter at least had his best mates to work and joke around with, while I only had a couple of new friends, Ayla, and him. I didn't have anyone to joke with except Ayla or my cats. I felt abandoned, with no one to lift my spirits. Peter didn't seem to know how to help and just tuned out when he was at home. Peter was able to ignore Ayla completely when I put her down to make dinner. She screamed as he watched the television.

He didn't seem to understand when I'd had enough of her and wouldn't offer to take her from me, so I'd always have to ask him, "Peter, can you take Ayla?" "Peter pick Ayla up will ya? Can't ya hear her screaming in front of you?" "Peter I know you've had a big day at work, but I've had a big day with OUR baby!" On and on it went, Peter never seemed able to take care of Ayla, and

I had assumed he'd be a great dad. He was overcome with fear of the responsibility of taking care of her. She didn't make attachment easy. So these were my thoughts on driving back to Perth.

Peter seemed very contrite when he opened the door and greeted me, but he promptly handed Ayla back to me, and she attached like a little greedy leech, sucking for all she was worth. Although I was happy to have my baby back, I knew things had to change for all of our sakes.

Peter finally realised I wasn't a super woman and that he had help care for Ayla, even if he was scared and she was screaming at him. We decided that I had to be out of the room or house so she couldn't smell my milk or see me. And, he would have to put up with the screaming as the neighbours had to do when he took her outside in the pram (which she hated) and walked her up and down the street. I took it upon myself to investigate why she was always so upset and needed to sit upright. I ploughed through every baby book I could find.

Boy, I would have loved to have had access to the Internet. The information I could have found! But as it was, books were great too, and books are still great! I came across gastric reflux in babies and so decided to try Gaviscon,® which is an antacid (Gaviscon Infant® is now available) and try her on that for a couple of days to see if it made a difference. It appeared to help, so the next step was to convince a physician that Ayla's problems were associated with reflux. I selected another new doctor, approximately my tenth, as I was trying to find one who would listen.

I brought Peter along, so the doctor wouldn't think it was just my neuroses. A couple of her previous physicians had wanted to put me on Valium and send Ayla to Ngala, where babies were sent (without their parents) to learn to sleep properly. As if that were Ayla's problem. Babies cry for a reason, not because they are being manipulative.

Peter came with me and didn't say anything, but he listened as I explained how difficult Ayla was and about the reflux (and

Gaviscon) and asked her to prescribe a stronger antacid. I also told her that I thought Ayla had a bladder infection and asked to have her urine checked. My veterinary nursing training was coming in handy; vets often had to be detectives and that's what I was doing. The doctor wasn't convinced, so I reminder her, "We're paying for it, and it can't do any harm. Please do what I've asked."

Not surprisingly, Ayla had a roaring bladder infection, and the stronger antacid worked! For the first time, Ayla slept for more than two hours at a stretch. It was miraculous; I got some desperately needed sleep, and so did Ayla. With the reflux and a bladder infection, she must have been in constant pain. Of course, she still suffered monthly ear infections until she had "grommets" implanted at sixteen months to relieve the pressure. What an enormous relief! Finally, some normalcy in our lives. Peter worked at building a relationship with Ayla, who finally started accepting him as her dad, and I felt as though I had crawled from deep underground.

It was whilst I was coping with Ayla that it occurred to me that I might have post-natal depression. I had ignored the question from the health care nurse, as I thought I would quickly snap out of it and that it was none of her business. When I answered the questionnaire accurately, based on how I actually felt, I realized that I was depressed. At the time I didn't want to be coerced into going to a physician who didn't know me. A doctor might prescribe anti-depressants, which I don't believe in.

I thought I just needed sleep and kept thinking hopefully that Ayla would learn to sleep. I didn't know where to go or who to turn to, but I especially didn't want anyone feeling sorry for me. I kept expecting to "snap out of it," not realising that women who have post-natal depression (PND) have little control over the way they're feeling.

I was a prime candidate for developing PND because of my traumatic, abusive childhood; unresolved issues of grief with my half-sisters and step-mum; the lack of family and community support; the lack of close friends; and Peter's frequent absences. I wasn't going to solve it on my own, and my strength and independence were hindrances.

Though I sought help from a counsellor for my anger (in reality, disguised sadness and grief) when Ayla was eight months old, I really needed help sooner—before my depression had deepened. If I had admitted to Peter that I really couldn't cope maybe he would have listened to me instead of thinking, "Oh Michelle can handle it, she's strong." In Peter's defence, he actually might have been suffering PND as well. Apparently ten percent of men and fifteen percent of women suffer from it, but we were both trying to shuffle through each day, praying Ayla would get better.

In addition to PND, I started to have panic attacks that left me feeling I had no control over my emotions. I was afraid to admit these attacks to anyone, even Peter. My panic attacks sometimes would start when I was sitting in the lounge room playing with Ayla. Overwhelmed by intense fear and apprehension that we were unsafe, I felt out of control and overcome with the need to escape the house. We'd go outside and sit on the grass for thirty minutes or so, until a new wave of fear and apprehension would force me back inside.

If this cycle repeated, I knew I was in trouble and would go shopping; not necessarily to buy anything but to connect to the outside world and escape the house. Often I'd have panic attacks about five in the evening, but at least by then Peter was home. Because I was embarrassed by my feelings, I'd go outside or start doing the wash, anything to stop those feelings. I often thought I was suffocating. I couldn't breathe properly or became lightheaded.

The worst was feeling as though I were looking at myself from a distance, detached from myself. It was so weird and disconcerting, but I didn't know what was happening, or how to get help. If I had admitted these feelings to Peter, or a friend, maybe I wouldn't have felt so isolated or lonely; but for me to admit I felt out of control was a huge obstacle. I wasn't about to announce that to just anyone; trust was an enormous issue. Living with an alcoholic dad, I had learnt that I couldn't trust my feelings to anyone. Rather than receiving support, I learnt to expect humiliation and ridicule. In spite of my self-education through Al-Anon about alcoholism, I had never learnt how to manage with a child who would bring out my inner self and those fears.

My panic attacks were horrible; the counsellor said they came from repressed emotions I had locked after the traumatic events of my childhood, and that fear was the driving force. I also suffered from amnesia, unable to remember going through certain events that my brother and sister can remember.

Having Ayla was the trigger point of these emotions. The fear was coming up through my subconscious, especially when I found myself in the same situations as when I was young. Mum and I were playing on the floor when my dad walked into the room. The panic attacks at dinner-time were related to the time my dad came home from work, and we'd sit down to eat dinner. Certain situations brought back the fear I still had of my dad—hidden in my subconscious—associating certain situations with massive fear.

My counsellor helped me understand my fear and suggested it would be a great idea to go to university, get out of the house, and do something for myself. Not only would it benefit me but benefit Ayla as well, as she was a very social little girl.

When Ayla was eighteen months old, I went to university which I had postponed while I was coping with her and suffering sleep deprivation.

Chapter 8

Changing Priorities

In 1996, I enrolled at Murdoch University to study sociology and psychology. This would be fun—I was looking forward to learning about these subjects in depth. Only through Peter's encouragement did I truly believe that I could get into a university. I felt that I wasn't smart enough to pass the entrance examination as I'd quit school just before I turned seventeen and hadn't challenged myself academically for ten years.

With Peter kicking me from behind, I took a course for mature students on how to pass exams. The course was great. I thoroughly enjoyed relearning how to write essays and increase my comprehension. My score on the university entrance exam was just over eighty percent, a bit higher than average. Not bad for a high school dropout!

Ayla was six weeks old and breast feeding when I sat the exam, so Peter brought Ayla and I breast fed her between exams. I was unbelievably stressed and felt woefully inadequate. I decided to give it a go. "So how did you do?" Peter asked. "It was hard, but I managed to reflect on my travels through Africa and apply them to one of the questions. Yeah, I think I passed!" "Fantastic! I knew you would be great." Inside, I still felt a failure, worried that I hadn't passed, and I was kidding myself that I could go to university at the ripe old-age of twenty-eight.

Months passed while I anxiously waited to learn if I had "got into" "uni". One morning, I heard the postie deliver something. When I opened our letter box up, I saw an important-looking letter from the university. "Wow, here it is!" I thought. I flung the letter at Peter, who asked, "Are you sure you want me to open it?" "Yes, yes, yes, open it! But I can't look." I couldn't stand the suspense. Peter didn't say anything at first, then said, "Yep, they've decided that oldies like you can go to university. Look, you got a great score. You should be able to take your first option." "Unreal, no way! Did they make a mistake? Are you sure that's what it says?" I was over the moon—my heart was beating so fast, and I didn't realise that I was so uptight. Fancy me getting into university on my first attempt!

My entrance to university was sealed, and I went on to study sociology and psychology part time for a year. It was hard; studying for a double degree, raising Ayla, and coping during Peter's frequent absences. My energy levels were at an all time low, and I didn't want to sink again into depression, so I deferred my degree in the interests of my health and my relationships with Ayla and Peter.

I was disheartened when I realized that the masters degree was required to practice psychology. That might require ten years, especially as I didn't know if that was my heart's true desire. I decided that my intelligence had been validated, and if I wanted, I could to go back to university.

Ayla was wonderful, and I cherished parenting, but had no thought of another child. Peter and I believed one child was enough, especially after my bout with postnatal depression and the recurring issues from my childhood. Having another child was farthest from our minds at this stage in our lives, and we never thought we'd ever have another.

But sometimes an event changes you dramatically, as it did us. In 1996, whilst I was writing about "Kinship, Marriage and the Family" in sociology and "Development of Self, Autonomy, Self-Concept, and Self Esteem" in psychology, the "boys" in the SAS continued their training. One exercise included night-time manoeuvres in Black Hawk helicopters near Townsville, Queensland. Townsville has a large Army presence and it was a convenient place for our boys to train with the helicopter pilots of the 5th aviation regiment.

On 12 June 1996, two helicopters collided during a night-time counter-terrorist exercise. Eighteen men were killed: fifteen SAS soldiers and three from the 5th Aviation Regiment; and twelve soldiers were injured. Later we heard miraculous accounts of survival, extraordinary acts of bravery, and the severe psychological scaring among the injured and those nearby.

With extraordinary bravery, soldiers repeatedly risked their lives to rescue wounded mates. We knew that one of Peter's closest friends was participating in the exercise, and we feared the worst. Peter cried as I've never seen him, thinking he had lost both his best friend and others that he knew well. Many good mates were lost that night; many families lost their dads or sons. Peter lost several good mates and, like many others, still bears unhealed psychological scars.

The Black Hawk accident affected Peter and me profoundly. We agreed that life was short, you never knew what would happen, and we decided to have another baby. Our beautiful baby girl, Kara, was born exactly ten months after the accident, on 12 April 1997. To our enormous relief, Kara did not scream nearly as often as Ayla had, and seemed more contented.

At the beginning of 1997 I decided social work would be easier to manage than psychology, so I started my degree there. I had Kara in April and was back at "uni" the week later. I was not sure how, but I was determined to have my cake and eat it too. Six months later, I decided it wasn't for me. Perhaps, I'd lost interest in trying to balance parenthood, university, and studying with Peter absent up to five months of the year.

My stress was building, and I wanted to be the best mum I could, but I knew I couldn't in these circumstances. My heart just wasn't in it. It was tough being an "army wife," raising two children, and being in university. Lack of sleep was a killer; I used to sleep in my car between lectures.

The worst was missing my younger sister's wedding in Melbourne on Anzac Day while Peter was in Kuwait. Our prime minister had promised "Our boys will be back by Anzac Day." They were scheduled to be in Kuwait for six weeks, but that stretched to three months, and many soldiers came home to very upset wives.

Going to Kuwait had been contentious from the beginning; Saddam Hussein planned to invade Kuwait and threatened to use chemical weapons. Peter said he'd trained vigorously to quickly inject himself with anti-chemical warfare vaccines and don his chemical protection suit. Initially, I was extremely worried, though the whole issue quickly blew over. Peter was extremely well trained and knew he could rely had his mates. But I worried every night of those three months and wanted him home.

Although studying helped to distract me, the stress grew unbearable. Once again, I postponed my education and concentrated on being a mum and wife for the remainder of 1997.

About the end of the year, following a much-needed rest, I started getting itchy to go back to university the following year. It may sound silly, but I was determined to get a degree and contribute to our family's finances. I had loved working at the vet's back in Melbourne and never thought I could be truly contented just being a mum. Although I wanted to be happy just being home, I was easily bored. I craved the bustle of working, being paid, and of being part of something larger.

Peter couldn't understand why I wanted to go back to "uni" and said it was fine if I stayed home. But he was sweet and promising to support me if I went back to university. After really considering my options, I decided being a teacher might be a great idea. I had considered this option before, so I took a chance and re-enrolled at a different university to become an early childhood teacher. I thought this degree would provide the best of both worlds. I could teach school from kindergarten up to grade seven but be home with Ayla and Kara during school breaks.

I took to early childhood education like a duck to water, and I thoroughly enjoyed the first year. I really loved the opportunity to enhance Ayla's and Kara's educations and loved my "two-week practicals," meeting kids and getting them excited about learning.

Education is one of my passions. Every child should reach his full potential and I was ensuring that our children didn't miss that opportunity. Richard Court was then premier of Western Australia, and I met him and his wife at the pre-primary where their daughter was a student while doing my "two-week practical." Their daughter was a sweetie, but I nearly suffered foot-in-mouth disease when meeting her parents.

Because the premier was casually dressed, I did not recognize him at first. I almost blurted, "Gee, you look like someone I know," but thank goodness my brain saved me from that blooper! I smiled and told him he had a lovely daughter. When I had met his wife previously, I had told her quite proudly that her daughter and I had dressed her little doll up and had to take off her clothes, etc., just as if I were chatting with one of the other mums.

To this day I think she reckons me of the most down-to-earth teachers she has ever encountered, and she seemed pleased that I had spoken to her about such mundane things as dressing her daughter's dolly. None of the other teachers spoke to her like that, and I never knew why they were all a bit anxious, until I met the premier. That was an interesting time.

Peter and I were happy with our life: we had two beautiful, intelligent, outgoing girls and we were managing my studies and Peter's army career. Life seemed to be smooth. We spoke often about how easier things were with me doing my teacher's degree, and how I would love to teach in Indonesia some day. Peter thought he might be able to be posted there with the army. Our future looked rosy.

I am usually extremely rational, although with an odd sense of humour. I don't usually believe that tempting fate causes negative outcomes. Even so, I wonder if I haven't been punished by the Gods because I didn't leave well enough alone. Peter is not superstitious, but even he believes we tempted fate when we decided to have a another child.

Peter took one look at me, and I was pregnant again. It was Christmas time, and as I started to eat my beautiful chocolates I gagged and felt nauseous. "Wow, that's the first time that's happened!" I thought, "Either I've got a tummy bug or I'm pregnant." Peter always thought if we had another child we would be tempting fate. Was he listening to his intuition? Did he feel like our life was going to change I wonder?

As I knew I was pregnant I didn't rush off to the doctor's for a test—trust me it's not like the first or second time you get pregnant—you know what you are in for! I felt intuitively that something was out-of-the-ordinary; perhaps I was having twins. My first ultrasound was in March 1999, when I was back into the swing of things at university.

There was a niggling doubt that I could ignore no longer. I told the doctor, a fantastic general practitioner, of my fear that something was amiss and requested an ultrasound. "I am not sure what it is, but I feel that something is not right. For peace-of-mind, I need to do this." "Sure, no worries," he replied, and a few days later I had an ultrasound.

"Michelle Wood," the nurse called in the waiting room. "Oh great, here we go," I thought to myself. As I by passed six other women waiting for ultrasounds, I smiled and thought positively about raising twins. As the ultrasound gel was squished over my belly, I wasn't anxious or worried. I had declined Peter's offer to come with me because I'd had many ultra sounds with my other two children and knew the routine. But what I wasn't prepared for was the look of surprise on the technician's face.

"Hang on a sec," she told me as she went out of the room to consult a colleague. Lying there, not really knowing what to think, I watched as her colleague came in and looked at my baby. I could see it definitely wasn't twins but didn't know what the problem was. The technician said, "We did a nuchal (neck) scan, which showed an increase of fluid. That may indicate your baby has Down's syndrome." "What did you say," was my stunned reply, "How could that be? I've got two healthy girls! How could I have a Down's baby?" "We don't know for sure, you'll need to have a chorionic villus sampling, a CVS," the technician told me, not unkindly.

Talk about a reality check! I'd gone in half-expecting twins and I've walked out with the very real chance of having a Down's baby. Wow! Sometimes, shit happens all too quickly for me. I mumbled thanks, signed papers for the CVS, and booked an appointment for the following week. I stumbled out teary-eyed not caring much about anything. As often happens in the army, Peter was away the following week, and I faced the CVS alone.

After two childbirths without drugs, I wasn't worried about the pain from the needle, but I was terrified that it might cause me to miscarry. After cleaning my abdomen with antiseptic and guided by ultrasound, a technician inserted a slender needle through my abdomen into the placenta. I felt a burning pain, as if my bladder was being ripped from my body. The pain ended before becoming unbearable. Not the most pleasant event, but not the worst.

It had been suggested that someone accompany me and drive me home, but I was alone. It wasn't that no one would have come with me, I didn't ask. Peter and I had kept the secret and hardly anyone knew that I was pregnant; that's the way we wanted to keep it. At that point, if I knew I had a Down's baby I might have opted to abort, though I knew that decision would weigh heavily on me and Peter for the rest of our lives.

I didn't want anyone putting their "two bobs" in telling us what we should, or shouldn't, do. The decision was ours alone, though being ignorant of Down's babies didn't help. I know I would have consulted many people, when I was ready, about the right course of action for our family. But mostly other Down's parents, books, and doctors, rather than well meaning friends and family.

I know they loved us, only wanted to help, but they didn't know any more about Down's babies than we did.

My only experience was with a gorgeous little Down's boy of about six to whom I used to teach swimming in Melbourne. Therefore I put all thoughts out of my head as to what my baby might or might not have and just rested until the girls came back.

The next few days went slowly by. I thought about my cells growing in the laboratory and whether my baby's chromosomes were normal. Not wanting to dwelling on the negative, I focused on my beautiful little girls and enjoyed the time I had. Reality caught up with me a couple of weeks later as I sat waiting for the doctor to tell me "the news." "Okay, Michelle, it's good news! Your baby's chromosomes are all in order; there's no extra chromosome-21, which there would be with Down's syndrome."

"Oh wow! That's great! Boy, what a relief!" I said, "But what about the extra fluid at the back of my baby's neck, what does that mean?" "Well, the high thickness measurement can be associated with congenital heart defects, but in the specialist's opinion, you have only about a two percent chance of having a heart baby. I wouldn't worry too much. Get in touch with your general practitioner; he'll book you in for an ultrasound at nineteen weeks, just to make sure everything is OK." "Oh! OK, thanks then. Hey, since you checked my baby's chromosomes, you know if I'm having a boy or girl, right?" "Yes, congratulations! You're having a girl," the doctor told me. "Thanks for everything then, doc, bye for now." I said, my head filled with joy at the thought of having another little girl.

If this kept up, I thought, we could have a basketball team. All thoughts of a Down's baby dissipated. Without dwelling too much on having a baby with a congenital heart defect—I didn't know how serious that could be—I got on with my life. University was going very well, and this was my best pregnancy yet. I felt great and could even think about my assignments and whilst on my two-week practicals.

At nineteen weeks of pregnancy I booked my ultrasound—with much foreboding, Exams were the same week, and I opted to finish those first. "Just in case," I thought, "I really do have a child with a heart condition? What should I do?" Miraculously, Peter was home, and he came with me. "Thanks, Michelle. I don't see anything wrong with your baby. Will you be home later, in case I need to phone?" "Yes, sure. We're going straight home now; thanks for everything," I said. "Fantastic," Peter said as he gave me a huge cuddle, jumping around excitedly. I felt a premonition that I couldn't quite name. Once home, I didn't have to wait long for her phone call. The doctor asked if I would mind coming in the following day so the cardiologist could do another ultrasound, "Just to make sure." But I knew in my heart that something was amiss.

Peter couldn't get time-off to come with me in the morning, and then he needed to be home to look after Ayla and Kara. So, I went alone. At the time, I had no idea what it meant to have a congenital heart defect. My only experience with a heart defect was a friend in high school. Lee had a hole in her heart, which she didn't seem worried about, and which didn't seem to stop her from participating in sports or running around in the school yard.

Lee announced one day she wouldn't be at school for a couple of weeks as she was having the hole in her heart repaired. She didn't seem worried or nervous about her surgery. When Lee returned, we admired her scar and told her it looked cool. We talked about how she felt, and what she ate at the hospital. I had a naive view that maybe my daughter would have a hole in her heart, but no big deal, right?

I was in for a major shock. I woke to just how serious some things can be. I wasn't prepared mentally; it was not how I had envisaged my life. I thought it couldn't happen to me; that stuff happens to others, not to me. I had already dealt with so much in my life, and Peter did also, with the recent Black Hawk disaster. We didn't need this.

Chapter 9

What's Congenital Heart Disease?

Driving myself to the hospital the next day I was full of dread and sick with nerves. My thoughts swirled with questions: what if they stuffed up the tests, and my baby does have Down's. What is the problem with her heart? I didn't know about childhood heart problems, and I didn't know what to think. But D-Day had arrived for me and my family and my time was up. My only hope was that "the problem" wasn't bad, and that I could deal with whatever news I received.

"Anyway, here goes," I thought as I met the cardiologist for the first time with my big, swollen belly. I felt out of my depth and for once didn't say anything sarcastic. He was lovely though and acted as though it was the most normal way to first meet someone. Same routine as yesterday's ultrasound. I had gel all over my belly, and waited with baited breath for him to speak. The doctor was looking for something only he could see.

Before I'd had much time to think, he found the heart problem. He was expert at examining a baby's heart in minute detail. My baby's heart just looked like a blob to me. If I had spent the next ten years looking, I don't think I could have seen all the vessels. But the doctor showed me anyway, and I looked very interested, although I really couldn't make out what he was showing me. I was impressed with the cardiologist's thoroughness and the compassion in his eyes when he turned and looked at me, but I was too scared to ask any questions.

He said "Okay, when you get up please come into my office. Your daughter has a very serious heart problem, and we need to talk." "Okay, alright," I managed to squeak out, terrified that if I said anything else I would break down. My heart felt like it was being squeezed from the inside out. I couldn't breathe properly and felt like my mouth had instantly dried out. I was shaking and trying hard to keep my chin up and not cry before he had the chance to explain just how serious my baby's heart problem was.

How naive to think that the worst heart problem was a hole! Still shaking, I entered the doctor's office, and he asked if I would like something to drink. "Yes, water please." It was one of those hot days that I usually love, but the air-conditioning was not coping with my nervous sweating. Rubbing my shaking hands together, I placed them in my lap.

> Your baby has a congenital heart condition, called truncus arteriosus. A congenital heart defect is a problem with the heart that is present at birth. It's nothing you've done or haven't done. It's just the luck-of-the-draw, and I am really sorry. Your pregnancy will have to be monitored closely to make sure the baby grows normally. We'll do a routine ultrasound at thirty weeks. Regular checkups will be necessary, but apart from that your pregnancy should be normal.

There was nothing in particular I had to do that was any different from my other two pregnancies. Of course, no alcohol was permitted, and it was essential that I rested and relaxed as much as possible ensure my pregnancy continued without any problems. I wasn't put on a special diet; this type of heart disease is not related to diet. Nor did I have to worry about my salt intake. Essentially I ate really well, but for the first time, chocolate made me sick Can you believe that? I wish chocolate still made me sick—I eat too much of it.

The other way this pregnancy affected me was to make me sad; I knew I was carrying a baby with a major heart defect. In spite of the cardiologist's assurance, I felt extremely guilty and fearful that I had done something to cause it. But the doctor was right; there is no known cause of congenital heart disease, and the mother is not to blame.

Our cardiologist advised me, "Your baby is quite comfortable right now inside your womb. Once she is born, we will see how well she does." "Will she be able to have a normal life?" I asked, worried that she wouldn't be able to keep up with her big sisters and not have a great quality of life. "Would it be better to terminate rather than have a baby with a massive heart problem?" "No, not at all, the heart problem isn't sufficient enough for you to terminate. Also, the hospital has policies that wouldn't allow you to do that because there's just not enough of a reason. After surgery, your baby should be fine and lead a pretty good life," he assured me, "Certainly able to run around, maybe not as fast as other children but at her own pace." So that was that.

Over the years, and lots of chats with other heart kid parents, I have learnt that they were given the option to terminate, so maybe it's a new law that's come in or only a law in West Australia. I am so glad I wasn't given the option; it's been a tough road, but not one I would have changed.

The doctor went on to explain what truncus arteriosus is. My baby would need surgery at nine weeks. The surgery had to be performed in Melbourne, at Royal Children's Hospital, widely known as RCH. There, world-class neonatal heart surgeons operated on babies as young as one day. My baby would also need the support of the RCH Intensive Care Unit (ICU) during recovery. There was no possibility of having the surgery in Perth, it was far too complex.

We would all be flown to Melbourne for the surgery when she was nine weeks old. The hospital would arrange the flights but could only fly Peter, myself, our new baby, and either Ayla or Kara to Melbourne and pay for accommodations for four family members. Peter had a chat with his Army colleagues, who blew us away with their generosity and caring attitude. Those big, tough guys have hearts of gold and covered the cost for Kara.

They also proved how fantastic they were over the course of the first five months of our baby girl's life. We really don't know what we would have done if they hadn't been as generous and understanding. Peter probably would have had to quit his job, as the kids and I needed him by our sides.

Thanking the cardiologist for his time, I walked slowly from his office after arranging an appointment for Peter to meet and talk with him. I was blown away by the news that my baby would have such a hard beginning to her life. Where's the justice in that? What had I possibly done wrong to cause this? Why me? How will I manage?

My other two children were fine. So what had gone wrong with this pregnancy? I felt my entire world caved in, and I couldn't really believe what was happening. Was I being punished for something? Hadn't I already gone through enough shit for ten people? I managed to hold myself together until I drove into our garage; then lost it, big-time. I felt like my heart had been ripped in half and my legs buckled when I tried to walk.

I cried and cried, sitting on the cold concrete. It was such a shock. One part of me was excited to be having another baby, and the other was terrified of having a baby with a major heart defect. The chances of losing her were about five percent, I had been told, but I was terrified of having a baby then losing her. I finally pulled myself together, walked into our house, and told Peter the news that he didn't want to hear.

The cardiologist had given me a couple of fact sheets about truncus arteriosus and about a support group called Heart Kids. We weren't connected to the Internet and had few sources of information. We took turns reading and re-reading the fact sheet about truncus, trying understand our unborn baby's condition.

We read that truncus arteriosus is a complex defect that occurs in less than one out of every 10,000 births, about one percent of all congenital heart disease. The two great arteries, aorta and pulmonary, share a single connection to the heart. Blood from both ventricles passes through a hole in the heart (called a VSD) into that single arterial trunk. The lung circulation is exposed to very high pressure and increased blood flow as a result of the VSD.

Our baby needed a conduit—a large tube and valve—to connect the right ventricle to the pulmonary artery and a patch to close the VSD. Surgery to repair the heart and blood vessels affected by truncus arteriosus is generally successful if done before two months of age. Left untreated, it is usually fatal during the first year of life.

Up to half of children with truncus also have DiGeorge syndrome, which is associated with a chromosome-22 disorder. If our baby did have DiGeorge syndrome, the effects could include a cleft palate, a characteristic facial appearance, and a low immune system that could lead to difficulty fighting infection She could also have learning disabilities, and social or emotional issues.

We also learnt that about one percent of babies have congenital heart defects, an average of six per day or 2,015 each year in Australia. It's the most common birth abnormality. Congenital heart defects are the leading cause of death for young children in Australia, accounting for more than thirty percent. This was news to me. I could hardly believe that we were having a baby with a heart defect. It was too daunting to comprehend, and there was a fifty percent chance of our baby would also have DiGeorge syndrome.

I felt like I had tempted fate, and the Gods were angry with me for not being satisfied with our life and our two beautiful little girls. Was it fate that we had this baby? Was it bad luck? Was it somehow meant to be? Was she a gift to us to teach us what we didn't appreciate in life? Once a parent has a child like this, he or she starts asking such questions.

After our initial shock, we set about naming our beautiful girl. Many nights and days were spent pouring over baby names and the book I especially liked was my friends' book of Irish names. I was very interested in the meanings, not just the names. Peter and I wanted her to have a name that would give her strength; so we poured over every name for its meaning and its sound.

We eventually found her first name, "Avelynn," meaning "life," but we australianised it to make it easier to understand and spell. Avelynn's middle name was far easier to choose, though none of us had heard it before. It's "Berneen," meaning "a hardy little bear," and we love it.

Coming to terms with the shock of having a heart baby took us quite a while. Not only did we have to adjust to what that might entail, we had to grieve over the loss over not having a normal baby. We worried how she would relate to her older sisters who were physically competent and capable in many ways. Understanding that I didn't cause her heart defect took a few months and was emotionally difficult. In my mind, I constantly replayed what I had done differently during this pregnancy and how I could have protected my child from heart disease. Our cardiologist had said it was nothing I did, or didn't do, but still I wondered.

Not only did I grieve the loss of a normal child, I grieved the loss of my university degree and the future I had envisaged with Peter and our other girls. Good-bye to teaching in Indonesia and farewell to the excitement I had anticipated of living and working in another country. It seemed to me that I had just recovered emotionally after having Ayla, my depression, my childhood, having Kara, and worrying about Peter serving in a war zone. Now I faced yet another monstrous challenge, and I often thought, "why me?"

Life sucked, although I knew I would fiercely love this baby, but I also knew she would change me forever. How could she not? The thought of having a third child was daunting enough without worrying whether she had DiGeorge syndrome and would be unable to fight off any infection from her surgery. The possibility was very real, but I tried to put it at the back of my mind. I also had to worry about her not making it through surgery. Roughly five percent of babies didn't.

Unknown complications were yet another lurking fear. Then I wrestled with telling Kara, who would be two-and-a half, and

Ayla, five, what was going to happen to their little sister. The issue was in how to approach the subject of Avelynn's surgery and keep my stress levels under control. The girls would manage if it did not seem too serious, but how could I do that?

I tried to approached this pregnancy with the realism that had served me well through many upheavals. I would keep my head up and my bum down and just get on with it. Take life one day at a time, try not to focus on the negatives, keep my stress levels down, eat well, and get enough sleep. Most importantly, I looked after my own well-being for the remaining twenty weeks of my pregnancy. Kara and Ayla were sources of happiness that kept me from spiralling back down to depression. Peter didn't go away, thank goodness. We needed him at home.

Managing my life was of the utmost importance. So I would be in control of something, I again postponed my degree, knowing I couldn't manage if I was at "uni". With all my worries, real or imagined, I couldn't concentrate on my studies. Our trip to Melbourne that November wouldn't have fit my class schedule. I remained optimistic about one day resuming my studies, but the realist in me knew it was an empty hope. But I had more pressing concerns; Avelynn birth was growing imminent.

My Little Red Head

Chapter 10

Heart Kids: a Whole New World

As I worried about the upheaval of Avelynn and her congenital heart defect, I remembered the pamphlet our cardiologist had given us and thought now was a great time to get in touch with the HeartKids organisation. Avelynn introduced us to a whole new world through our involvement in HeartKids. We discovered a great support organisation with fantastic parents who, like Peter and I, shared the trials and tribulations of having heart kids. HeartKids not only provides support, but also strives to raise awareness and funding of congenital and acquired heart disease in children.

I was nervous ringing up the organisation at first, but within moments was crying into my phone to the family support person of HeartKids. She was a complete stranger, but with her first few comforting words I knew she understood what I was going through better than my well-meaning friends and family. I didn't have to explain how upset and terrified I was; she already knew. I realized while speaking to her that I didn't have to struggle on my own, and could gain strength from her's and other's experience raising a child with heart disease.

Though I didn't go to the coffee mornings at Princess Margaret, (the local children's hospital) or become involved with many other parents before Avelynn's surgery, I spoke with other parents who's kids that had truncus arteriosus, the same as Avelynn. It was a source of comfort to know we weren't the only ones who had a child like that. I remember there were two parents that I spoke to, and they were great sharing their experiences of living with their child with truncus. It was all positive, and when I asked about any negative experiences, they said, "No, it was all pretty good." But when I asked if were other truncus babies that had grown up they said, "There's only two of us."

As truncus only represents one percent of congenital heart disease, I believed when they said it is very rare. I spoke to one mum in particular a couple of times, whose daughter was around eight years old. The mum explained how her daughter had done very well with her second heart surgery. "Wow, that's great!" I said, "I shouldn't be so worried about Avelynn's surgery."

We discussed how children with truncus have a part called a conduit which replaces their missing Pulmonary Artery and part of the vessel. Sadly, the conduit doesn't grow with them and must be replaced between the ages of five and eight years, depending on how each child is doing. Then they usually need another conduit replacement as teenagers.

This fascinated me, and I thought to myself, "Wow, they're given a spare part." I visualised the hospital stocked with jars of spare parts or some weird thing. Yuck, I didn't want to take that train of thought. But I suppose people donate their vessels, and that's one of the uses for them, for which I am eternally grateful; it gave Avelynn back her life. HeartKids were fantastic and a great support to me during my last twenty weeks of my pregnancy, just as they are to numerous parents and grandparents of children with congenital or acquired heart disease.

Avelynn's Birth

With my advancing pregnancy I couldn't help reflecting on the births of Ayla and Kara. Both girls were born in the fantastic atmosphere of the Family Birthing Centre, a home-like maternity care facility at the main maternity hospital in Perth. My birthing experience with Ayla and Kara was incomparably better than typical maternity hospital with monitors and strangers witnessing the birth. I was very fortunate to have the same midwife for Ayla and Kara, and I hoped Connie could deliver Avelynn as well.

I was able to give birth to Ayla and Kara in the birthing centre because those pregnancies had no complications. Connie—our midwife—was experienced, registered, had completed a post-graduate midwifery program, and was fantastic!

At the Birthing Centre, Peter could sleep in the double bed, with our baby asleep between us or in her little cot, whichever we chose. The atmosphere was relaxed; almost our home away from home. The furnishings were comfortable, including easy-chairs, our own air-conditioning, en-suite shower and toilet, and even a private garden. Peter and I had extremely strong feelings about the holistic approach to childbirth; it will always be one of the most magnificent times in my life.

I didn't have any pain killers, only lavender to sniff and some homeopathic drops to ease my anxiety. We only had Connie helping us. Peter got on brilliantly, which was great! We had the option of inviting friends, but we only wanted each other and our fantastic midwife. Some may think that I was crazy; what, no pain killers? And there were a couple of times when I too thought I was crazy not to have something.

Where I would give birth to Avelynn became a very contentious issue. Because of Avelynn's congenital heart defect, we were told I had to give birth at the hospital. Regrettably, there was no question about being allowed to have Avelynn at the birthing centre. We were told that under no circumstances is any mum allowed to give birth at the centre if there is any complication with the mum or the baby.

I was very disappointed, but understood. I couldn't risk Avelynn even though the birthing centre was attached to the main hospital. This decision didn't sit well with me. I had desperately wanted to go to the birthing centre, just as I had with Ayla and Kara. The hospital simply would not allow it because of the many risks. She might not be breathing properly, or at all, or they could have missed something in the ultrasound. I knew logically that anything could have happened, but I grieved for what my heart wanted but could not have.

When I was thirty-five weeks pregnant, I informed my obstetrician that I only wanted Peter, myself, and a midwife in the delivery room during Avelynn's birth. 1,000 people could be on the other side of the door, but they were not to interfere, help, or come into the room while I was giving birth. Peter understood this, and I told him if he wanted to be around then he would have to guard the door. "But, oh my, that isn't allowed," the obstetrician said, "No way."

I have a fairly strong personality, but at my best, I use humour to blunt my words. But when confronted, I can become ugly and impossible to reason with. Regrettably, I clashed horns with my obstetrician, telling her that I would stay home and simply turn up in an ambulance if she didn't let me have my way. I reasoned with her, pointing out that anyone we might need was only seconds away, but that I didn't need any help giving birth to my child. I told her that I wasn't on show and neither was Avelynn just because she had a rare heart disease.

We went back and forth for a couple of weeks. I wouldn't give up on my ideal way of giving birth, which I believe was my right, and no one was going deny me that. The doctor's first priority was Avelynn's safety, and she wouldn't concede. She was a specialist in abnormal pregnancies and complicated births, which she thought mine would be, but I was adamant that it was "my way or the highway."

They had a board meeting to talk about me. I was one of the most stubborn mothers they had ever encountered. They agreed to meet us half-way. The medical staff would wait in the hall way until I had given birth, then they would come in. I wouldn't have minded if she had assured me that it would be only her and the midwife, I would have conceded that, but she came with other hospital members who all wanted to be there in case of difficulty. I felt like I was forced to choose between just the midwife and Peter, or the whole kit-and-caboodle.

I was certain there would be no complications with the birth of Avelynn, and I was very confident in my ability and in Peter's support.

At forty weeks, I still hadn't shown any signs of giving birth. Lots of Braxton Hicks contractions—false labour pains—but nothing more. I felt great and continued to walk around the small hill near our house to enjoy the beautiful panoramic views of the ocean and the surrounding area. I had looked after myself so well, taken my supplements, and eaten really well. I felt fantastic. It was my best pregnancy, but it was also the hardest emotionally. My baby might have to fight for her life from the moment she was born.

At forty-one weeks, I had an appointment with my lovely doctor. She really was lovely, just not used to stubborn mums. Under no circumstances she said, was I allowed to go to forty-two weeks pregnant. She wanted me induced—a method that artificially stimulates childbirth—the following day. What? No way was I going to allow that! "Come on baby Avelynn, get out, little sweetie," I remember telling her sternly, "Come on, you can do it! We don't want any drugs, or lots of doctors."

My doctor said, "We can let you go home, but if you don't have her tonight, I want to see you in my office tomorrow. First though, I will put some gel on to your cervix and see if that helps start contractions. Okay?" That was a simple procedure, but the doctor was surprised; I was already dilated three centimetres. Going home, I wished with all my might that I would go into labour, but I was also afraid. I had given birth to Kara in just sixty-five minutes and was a bit nervous that this would be the same.

That night I got my household organised and took Peter shopping with the girls. I viciously guarded my shopping trolley from Peter, to swing off when my contractions came. "Shit! Maybe they are real," I thought, ignoring them anyway as I continued shopping. A few people looked at me but I only smiled and waved them away. Peter asked several times if I wanted to go home, but I said, "No I'm fine, let's just get on with it; we need food in the house!" As I was lying in bed that night, waiting for something to happen, I thought that when I did go into labour, our lives would be changed forever. I had given Ayla and Kara an extra big cuddle each and wished them sweet dreams.

At midnight, my stomach went into a horrendous contraction, but all I could think about was how tired I was and that I didn't really feel up to giving birth. I tried to ignore it, and started to roll over without waking Peter. Wham! Another one hit me, which I couldn't ignore. The moment we had been anticipating arrived with excitement and trepidation.

I grabbed my bag, Ayla, and Kara. Peter drove us to a friend's who would look after the girls. Peter was having a gab while I was swinging off the door frame, trying to get his attention. My contractions were so fierce, that I couldn't speak; I was kind of squeaking and waving frantically at Peter. Finally, he noticed and we hot-tailed it out of there, arriving at the hospital ten minutes later. Now, my contractions were only one or two minutes apart. "Crickey," I thought, "this is fast!"

Peter tried to rush me, but I had to swing off the hospital fence every few feet for support as another contraction hit me. If I would have had my way, I would have given birth on the footpath; it was nearly impossible to walk. So I waddled, half hanging onto Peter, half swinging off the fence, and somehow made it into the hospital. At this point, I could neither walk nor sit, and I wanted Peter to carry me; but he said he was sorry and he couldn't do that. I waddled, hanging onto the hospital wall and Peter, until I collapsed near a chair. The midwife checked me and could hardly believe I was already dilated ten centimetres.

She said something about never seeing anyone walk when they were dilated ten centimetres, which meant I had been in intense labour at my friend's place, in the car, and whilst hanging onto the hospital fence. I was about to give birth. It was almost a comedy, and I might have laughed, if not for the pain.

Waddling into the birthing room, I took one look at the specially designed birthing bed and decided to give it a miss. It sure didn't look comfortable. Now desperate, I homed-in on a chair, and kneeled on the floor in front of it. For the moment, I was quite happy with that position; I could rest my head and arms. There was nothing else in the room, unlike our suite in the birthing centre, which was set up for basically giving birth in any position that took your fancy—except for sitting on the toilet—a big no-no.

I wasn't comfortable and I was basically having Avelynn when I arrived. There was no time to change my mind, as much as I wanted to. I couldn't move; as most women know, once you're in position to give birth, you stay put. So there I was, leaning over that bloody chair and sooooo uncomfortable, but I couldn't move, and there was no time for drugs.

When Avelynn pushed her head out she broke my coccyx—my tail bone. I yelled at the nurse, "Hey! What are you doing to me? You're really hurting me!" The nurse was confused, saying "I've done nothing! I'm doing nothing! I'm not even touching you!" I didn't believe her and turned around to check. She standing a metre away, just holding her hands in the air. She said, "Your baby has her eyes open! She's twisting her head from side-to-side as much as she can to get a glimpse of the new world around her and see what was going on." "Unbelievable!" I thought, "You're one hell of a crazy baby."

So there I was leaning over the chair and basically refusing to go any further. I thought, "To hell with this! I've had enough, I'll just rest for a while." The midwife said very sternly, as though talking to a naughty child, "Come on, Michelle! You're going to have to push. Come on, push! There's no time for mucking about."

Peter yelled at me to push her out and I thought, "Okay for you two! You haven't got a bloody broken tail bone." But they didn't realise what had happened, only that I wasn't cooperating. When I homed in on the chair, I had no idea that it would be so uncomfortable giving birth in that position. I thought I knew what I was doing. But one lives and learns, doesn't one?

The chair didn't support me very well, nor support my stomach. So there I was, my arms nearly breaking, hanging on to the chair with grim determination. Of course, I had to push little Avelynn out, and I don't know who screamed the loudest. The nurse was yelling at me, "Come on, Michelle! You have to push her out. She's going blue!' Peter was yelling at me as well, and I knew I had gotten myself into hot water, but I was in agony. Finally an hysterical note in Peter's voice, yelling at me "She's going blue—push her out," had the requisite effect. I gave an almighty push and screamed blue bloody murder, but out she came.

I barely had time to look at Avelynn and register that she had gorgeous strawberry blonde hair. She was screaming her head off, and I was in agony with my poor broken coccyx. No more chairs for me for a while. Unfortunately, my broken coccyx probably had a lot to do with the position I was in, and that I had broken it before in childbirth. Oh, well! What mums sacrifice! From the first real contraction to holding her in my arms, my labour was only fifty-five minutes. Avelynn had arrived with a bang.

Her attitude at birth—opening her eyes and looking around before she was fully born—told me she had attitude to burn and wasn't afraid to use it. Her attitude toward life continues to this day. Once she decides to do something, there's no stopping her. Avelynn is a unique and determined individual; she will stare into the eyes of fear as if to say, "See if I care. Bite me! "

There she was, a beautiful little strawberry blonde girl. I barely had time to register just how gorgeous she was when the nurses wanted to whisk her straight off to the intensive-care unit (ICU). First, I needed a quick cuddle and demanded to hold Avelynn. Once I held her, I didn't want to let her go, but the nurses were insistent. "No, no, no! She's got a heart condition and we have to take her to intensive care!" I couldn't blame them for wanting to quickly check her out. She had a rare heart defect and was a strange, mottled colour with a tinge of blue. Reluctantly, I let her go to the ICU ensure she was breathing okay and wasn't distressed. Peter didn't need to be asked; he followed her to the ICU.

The lovely midwife checked my blood pressure and was surprised to find it back to normal, "Wow! I can't believe your blood pressure is normal only fifteen minutes after giving birth. I bet we won't be able to get you to stay in bed and rest will we," she said. "No, not really," I replied. My midwife was quite impressed with my positive attitude and that I appeared fit, which helped immensely. This was a breeze; it was my best pregnancy.

I told the midwife, "Come on, you've got to get this placenta out of me! Come on get it out!" She massaged my stomach and pushed down on my uterus until the placenta came out. I was covered in muck from head to toe;. Giving birth really is a messy business, no matter what you do.

Avelynn made a real mess, but as I waddled into the shower I was overjoyed that Avelynn appeared to be so lively. It was a wonderful experience for the three of us and pushed from my mind all thoughts of the looming heart surgery. My focus shifted, and I was overpowered by the desire to be with Avelynn. It was about half-past one in the morning, and I hadn't slept, but I felt alive and wonderful. Donning my comfortable nightie and slippers, I waddled quickly down the hall. A nurse followed, worried that might I pass out.

I was delighted to see Peter with Avelynn as I sat next to him and gave her my breast. The experience of breast-feeding Ayla and Kara for a total of three years served me well, and Avelynn got a good feed. Peter told me they had put her in a little oxygen capsule when they first bought her to ICU, because her oxygen saturation was only eighty percent, far below the normal level of one hundred percent. The congenital heart defect caused her oxygen-rich and oxygen-poor blood to mix. She would continue to struggle until she had surgery at nine weeks to repair her heart. There we were, with our beautiful baby, Peter looked proud, but probably wondered, as most dads do, how the hell I had managed to give birth.

My endorphins were still acting as natural pain-killers, enabling me to tolerate my poor, broken coccyx and the rest. I was fixated on Avelynn and kept asking the nurses how she was doing. They seemed amazed that she was going so surprisingly well, but continued to monitor her oxygen saturation through a miniature sensor clipped to one of her tiny toes. Avelynn was a gorgeous little baby, but her colour was very motley because of her heart condition. She was ours, and we thought she was beautiful.

Objectively, I suppose, newborns aren't the most attractive babies, with their heads still squished from the birth canal. I guess my head wouldn't look great if that happened to me. To us she was beautiful and gorgeous.

In spite of my broken coccyx, we left the hospital about twenty-four hours later. That may surprise some, but when you've got a great bed at home, a great husband, and two other kids who couldn't wait to meet their little sister, back home you go.

Chapter 11

Home, Sweet Home

Arriving home with Avelynn was absolutely amazing, as it always is with a new-born. They are magical, with that new-born smell and you want to protect and nurture them, and keep forever from harm. It is always overwhelming to be totally responsible for a tiny, helpless baby who can't even hold up her head; and even more so with Avelynn. Any new child changes family dynamic, but with Avelynn it was more: she totally changed our lives and changed all of us. We were forced to change as our perceptions were challenged on every front. Avelynn forced us to change and grow whether or not we wanted that. Not only did I have a third child to contend with—and that's difficult—but Avelynn was special. It was up to me to tackle head-on the issues of having a heart kid.

I had no experience with "heart" babies or chronically ill children, and I felt an overwhelming sense of responsibility. My cardiologist was wonderful and caring. He said that if I couldn't cope with Avelynn, or was worried about absolutely anything, I should phone him or the hospital. He said I could even be admitted to the hospital if I needed extra support.

As her mum, the challenges of Avelynn's condition forced me to rethink many of my perceptions of myself as a parent. No longer was I the confident mum of five and two year-old girls, but the inexperienced mum of a baby with heart disease. I was afraid to pick her up; afraid she would pass away in her sleep.

I constantly checked her breathing, took her temperature, and changed her clothes. I was scared to wash her in case it became physically overwhelming for her, and I was terrified when she cried, leaping to attend her at the slightest whimper. Friends who came over were put through a quick quarantine search and questioned at the front door. If I found, or even suspected, any illness, they were turned away. We explained that we were sorry, but they could come back another time, as I was extremely worried about her catching any germs before her heart surgery.

Although I learnt to live with this fear of losing her, at times I let it pour out, crying and crying until I had no more tears. I cursed the injustice of having a child with heart disease. I grieved the loss of a normal baby, and having quit university and the possibility of never completing my degree. The magnitude of my situation sometimes got the better of me, and I still had to manage my other children, who were very dependent on me.

Overall, we kept our spirits up, and maintained a positive attitude in front of our friends and children, that Avelynn would be okay. We concentrated on bringing her home after surgery, getting ready for Christmas, and making a new start in 2000. Above all, we wanted to remain positive and hopeful.

We had nine weeks at home with Avelynn before flying to Melbourne for her heart surgery, and I wanted everything to be positive, joyous, and peaceful. I concentrated on "why not" rather than "what if," and tried not to let sadness rule me. When I felt sad, angry, or guilty, I would try to stop and focus on giving Avelynn the best for those nine weeks. If I did that, I knew it something was beneficial for us both. Nine weeks is a long time when it is your entire life, and I think our family made the best of that time.

We took Avelynn and let her look at the trees blowing in the wind, walked along the beach, and listened to the waves crash, patted the cats and dogs, played with wonderful toys, and experienced many textures, sights, and sounds. Outside, she could lie in her pram and watch the beautiful shadows and shapes of the leaves blowing gently in the breeze, or listen to the dogs chase Ayla and Kara around the backyard.

Avelynn especially loved it when Ayla and Kara spoke or sang to her. She would swivel her head and try to follow their voices with her eyes. There always seemed to be a positive vibe around her as she experienced a lot of love, happiness, and bucket-loads of attention.

I remember those weeks with great fondness; they helped forge unbreakable bonds among Peter, me, and Avelynn, and among Avelynn, Ayla, and Kara. It's a time Peter and I often reflect on warmly. Avelynn knew without doubt that she belonged to a family that truly loved her, and we're sure that helped her survive the hospital.

Even though Avelynn was born with a major heart defect, she had a fantastic first nine weeks of her life and even got to sleep tucked up against Peter or me, just as Ayla and Kara had done. We didn't have any issues with that. We thought it was a great way to raise our kids. This hasn't done them any harm; they eventually decided to move out on their own.

Not only did Avelynn get to cuddle Peter and me at night, but for most of the day as well. From from the moment Avelynn came home, we took up residence in the lounge room. Our spare mattress became a permanent fixture in front of the TV. It wasn't a nuisance, but an essential part of parenting.

Avelynn took so long to breast feed it was a way I could relax. Ayla and Kara often laid down next to us, and watching TV took on a whole new meaning. I had to lie down—my broken tail bone was still incredibly painful. We watched the Wiggles from this angle, that angle, and the other. Usually, we watched the Wiggles, Playschool, Barney, and the Hooley Dooleys, or movies that we hired. Breast-feeding Avelynn was a full time job. Occasionally I'd yell out to Peter, "Can you get me a drink, please?" Or "Peter, I need something to eat. I can't move, Avelynn's gone to sleep on me." That was the fun bit. Often, Ayla and Kara would fall asleep as well, and so would I.

Feeding Avelynn occupied a large percentage of my time; I learned that babies with heart disease tire very easily while they're feeding, and Avelynn could only handle a small amount at one time. I had to feed her frequently to ensure she put on weight.

The extra work of Avelynn's heart made her burn more calories, therefore she needed more food than a normal baby. This was one of the biggest concerns I had, ensuring that she gained enough weight between weekly weigh-ins with the community nurse. Many babies with serious heart conditions don't put on much weight. Avelynn's weight wasn't cosmetic, it was vitally important. Healthy weight babies have better survival chances during and after heart surgery. Most of the time I wasn't worried; she was gaining weight, wasn't going blue, or showing other signs of distress. The stress regarding her weight wasn't fun but I had to ensure we were fattening her up nicely for her surgery.

At first, I produced so much milk that I could have fed triplets—I offered my milk around as a treat. Ayla and Kara were quite enthusiastic at first, but soon rejected the "funny tasting milk." Peter wouldn't have a bar of it, and said it was disgusting. I hated to see a good thing go down the drain, so I tried it on my beautiful Burmese cats, but even they weren't interested. There was no need to store my milk as no one else was going to look after her or come within cooee of her. I didn't know if she would ever take a bottle, and it just seemed too hard to store it all.

I mastered breast feeding Avelynn on the mattress, watching the "Wiggles" and relaxing, while coping with Ayla, Kara, and the cats. The cats wanted to get in on the act and sit on me or Avelynn. More importantly, Peter and I had started a ritual of pigging-out on garlic bread, fetta rolls slathered with butter, and other bakery delights for Ayla and Kara. Mmm, yum, it was mouth watering, especially when still warm from the baker's oven. We had in the back of our minds the fear that we might not bring our baby back home, which was the hardest thing to contemplate. So we set about enjoying the finer things in life, including delicious delights from the bakers.

We knew we had a five percent chance of losing her during surgery, plus an unknown chance of losing her to post-surgery complications. We did not want to think about it. That was just from her truncus repair. Little did we know then, that she also had pulmonary hypertension—high blood pressure in her lungs—which would add considerably to her risk. We were still blissfully unaware of the drama about to unfold once we flew to Melbourne; like most, I had never heard of that disease.

Peter and I didn't know much about heart conditions either; the closest I got to it was a high-school friend who'd had heart surgery. She seemed fine, was a great friend, and had survived open-heart surgery. We had all admired her scar, thinking it was pretty cool, but that was extent of my knowledge of heart kids. Even after we knew about Avelynn's heart condition, our knowledge was limited to a few chats with the cardiologist.

Now, I know that a lot of children have heart problems and not all survive. Unless you know a child, friend, or relative who's had it, childhood heart disease is not common knowledge. The public seems generally unaware of heart problems in children; it's seldom discussed. Unfortunately, there is a fear-factor associated with heart disease in children. Not so much among the parents, but the fear in your friends faces when you're talking about the possibility your heart kid could die. It's a taboo subject. Since I've had Avelynn, a lot of people have told me they've lost a child to heart disease, but often had told no one outside their immediate family.

No one likes to think that children die from heart disease, but it claims more children ten years and younger than any cause except car accidents. I met one woman who had lost her little girl at about five years old, and she told me that hardly anyone understood how that could happen. Heart Kids is a support group that sponsors bereavement coffee-mornings where parents and friends get together once in a while to catch up and share their common bond. It is food for the souls of those who attend.

Avelynn's cardiologist, Dr. Luigi D'Orsogna, wanted to see her every week to check her weight and that her condition did not worsen. If the need arose, or I was worried, I could call him or the hospital at any time. At the end of nine weeks, we were thrilled that our beautiful little baby had reached the massive, unbelievable weight of five kilogrammes. She had done us and herself proud. Most parents would be happy to get their normal babies to five kilogrammes in nine weeks, much less those with a heart condition. Avelynn also had the chance to show off her heart; the video of her echocardiogram was used at university for training doctors in Western Australia. I don't know if her video was used for training in Melbourne or the Eastern states, as the locals call it. I'm sure they had their own babies to video—other little stars showing off their hearts to hundreds—but I know they used Avelynn's video (she was referred to simply as "a truncus baby") for training in Western Australia.

Luigi D'Orsogna also used Avelynn to help train some of his medical students. I got a phone call from Luigi, "Hi, Michelle. I hope you wouldn't mind bringing Avelynn in so a few medical students can listen to her heart, That will help them become more proficient at listening to an abnormal heart beat." "Peter, do you think we should bring Avelynn in so some medical students can listen to her heart?" "Yeah, okay. Sure, sure anything to help future heart kids."

Off we went, proud to help out and show off our baby girl. Ayla and Kara came with us; Luigi was interested in listening to their hearts to check if either had a heart murmur. We trooped into his office, a little nervous and anxious, hoping Avelynn behaved herself so all the students could get a listen. Apparently a lot of children with congenital heart disease aren't diagnosed. It's difficult for doctors who haven't had that specific training to detect abnormal heart beats in very young children.

We were glad to be helping out and doing our bit for heart kids. All the students had to wash their hands and hardly spoke to us—perhaps they were a little nervous, too. At this early stage, we did not know if Avelynn had DiGeorge syndrome. Children with DiGeorge don't have fully effective immune systems, which could be fatal in Avelynn's case because heart surgery caries such a huge risk of infection.

So the medical students were being very cautious, wore masks, and carefully washed up. Avelynn put up with it, although I am sure she was too tired to do much. That was the thing about her, she didn't complain much and couldn't work up a fearsome, blood-curdling yell like most new-borns can emit without so much as blinking. Avelynn didn't have much energy, and the energy she did have she put toward feeding and gaining weight.

Apart from the few visits to our cardiologist, breast feeding Avelynn, and pigging-out on yummy bakery delights, we tried our best to keep up a normal routine for Ayla and Kara. We endeavoured to get Ayla to preschool (the year before One). If she got to school on time, great; if not, bad luck. If she didn't get there at all, no big deal. Though we tried our best to keep a schedule, we often ate at irregular times and fed the animals when required.

One of the best moments we had was surprising Ayla and Kara with a special present. I said, "Come on, Ayla and Kara, I've got a present for you!" While I was pregnant, I had painted T-shirts with, "I'm a big sister" on the front of them. The shirts looked fantastic, and the girls were excited and proud to get them. A couple of other friends bought presents for Ayla and Kara and the girls' faces just lit up when they saw their presents. It wasn't just Avelynn receiving presents. It was a bit like Christmas in September. It was brilliant, and we loved it!

Chapter 12

Flying to Melbourne

The day had finally arrived. We couldn't do anything to delay it, we had to go with the flow. We had organised friends to look after our dog, fish, and house; it was all a go. We packed the kids, and then dropped off our beautiful Burmese cats, Khan and Mungo, at the cattery. Little did we know that we wouldn't see them for a month. We thought we would be gone for ten days, tops, which included being in the hospital.

Flying to Melbourne was terrible! Normally I would have been very happy flying in to see my relatives, but not this time. Fortunately, Avelynn was stable enough to go without oxygen support, and we didn't need a nurse or a doctor to accompany us on the flight. That surprised us a bit, as we knew she had low oxygen in her blood, but it was not low enough for concern.

Peter and I tried to be brave, but we were absolutely terrified that something would go wrong with Avelynn on the flight to Melbourne. Not only did we have to worry about Avelynn, but we had the girls, who were hard enough to deal with on the four-hour flight.

Getting on the plane, I was so scared that my heart was thumping. I asked Peter, "You know, this is it! Wow, how are we going to manage?" Peter patted my hand in reply as if to say, "Don't worry too much, let's just get over this plane flight." He was great and looked after Ayla and Kara, with help from the wonderful Qantas staff, who entertained the girls.

I nursed Avelynn, but the lower oxygen levels on the plane made it harder for her to breathe, and she was very sleepy. I tried to keep her nuzzling away at the breast milk, hoping that would keep her lungs open and ease her breathing a bit. During the last hour of the flight, I was extremely concerned because Avelynn had turned a hideous motley colour from lack of oxygen. Touching down in Melbourne was an incredible relief;.

Our local hospital had organised everything; we even had a paid hire car that we had the use of for two days. We stayed with my mum, who lives in the beautiful Yarra Valley seventy kilometres east of Melbourne. It's takes about ninety minutes to drive to mum's place through Ringwood and Lilydale, and along the Warburton highway to Millgrove. We were there in the spring, and it was beautiful, with wildflowers, mild weather, and the wonderful aromas of eucalyptus, boronia, and tea-trees.

The scents reminded me of when I had lived there with mum, so it was a bit of a home-coming for me. "The Valley," as the locals call it, welcomed us with its beautiful spring smells, sunshine, and warm weather. It was the perfect place for us to spend a day relaxing with my family before we were due at the hospital.

My Melbourne family all turned out to greet us: mum (of course) along with my sisters, Sharon and Kimberley, and my brothers, Rowen and Adam. Adam, who lives in the USA, had flown in with his wife Elizabeth and both their children especially to see us. It was absolutely fantastic to see them all together.

Adam is younger than me, and I would wrestle and fight with him when we were children. We shared a secret language and a dry wit. Whenever we're together, we act like total idiots. It was so great to see and banter with him in a way that no one else shares.

Everyone was saying, "Oh, it's great to see you and meet Avelynn!" "Look at her—doesn't she look so cute!" And, "Gee, where does she get her hair colour?" Avelynn has strawberry-blonde hair and green eyes, unlike anyone else in the family. Peter said his grandfather, Dal, had red-coloured hair and they used to call him Red. I've only seen an old black and white photograph, so who knows his true hair colour? We just think Avelynn's hair and eye colour are very special.

It was great to catch up with everyone, and we all fondly remember sharing that special day. We'd decided to have a day out and headed up to the Upper Yarra Reservoir, a bit past East Warburton and about twenty minutes from mum's house. We shared a fantastic picnic ground at the Upper Yarra lake, which supplies water for Melbourne. It was perfect for the beautiful, sunny, spring weather we were having.

Adam took it upon himself to wrestle single-handedly with all his nieces and nephews: Ayla, 5, Kara, 2-½, Bianca and Hayden, both 4, and Tamara, 9. The kids had no sooner pinned Adam, than my mum and, to our shock, even grandma decided to join in. "Grandma what are you doing?" We shouted, "Don't break anything!" It was a real hoot watching our families come together and have lots of fun. We spent most of the day there enjoying a typical Aussie BBQ—flies and all.

The next day we said good-bye to Adam and his family, who flew back to the USA. They gave Avelynn an beautiful, snow-white angel teddy-bear with white, glossy wings and a serene face. The angel bear had their blessing (they are highly religious) so it seemed appropriate that we said angel bear was like Avelynn's guardian angel. Adam and Elizabeth asked us to take it to the hospital, so we hung angel bear up in the ICU to remind us of its special meaning.

Adam and Elizabeth started a prayer chain for Avelynn when they arrived home. They were very caring and said it was the least they could do. We were astounded that they set up a prayer chain on the Internet and recruited hundreds and hundreds of strangers to pray for our dear daughter.

Avelynn had struck a chord with many people and the love and energy that we felt flowing to Avelynn on the day of her surgery through the prayer chain was beautiful! I hoped the universe was listening, and that the positive energy flowing from their prayers would reach Avelynn.

Our main concern was keeping Avelynn healthy and ready for heart surgery. We had to be careful that no one, not even our family, approached her if they had any sign of illness.

Chapter 13

Royal Children's Hospital

With heavy hearts, we said a sad farewell to my family, who cried over us like a water works. The hardest part was leaving Ayla and Kara behind with my mum, wondering if they would ever see Avelynn again. In the morning, she would have a lot of procedures at the Royal Children's Hospital in Melbourne, and the girls weren't allowed to come with us. If all went well, she would have heart surgery the next day.

I couldn't bear the thought of Avelynn dying, but it was a possibility. Ayla and Kara had sad little faces when we left. The last I heard was my mum—their grandma—telling them what a wonderful time they would have at the zoo in a couple of days, and how she needed their help to feed her dogs and cats. Kara was only two and a half, and had never spent a night away from me. I was mostly worried about her. They barely knew my mum, but I tried to think positively. I remembered how much fun they had at the reservoir the day before and hoped they were forming a close bond.

We checked into our hotel, where we would be staying for two nights, only 100 metres from the Royal Children's Hospital. The following morning, we arrived at the hospital early for Avelynn's procedures. We were fairly clueless. Neither of us had much experience with hospitals, how they worked, nor did we know much about the procedures.

We had only been in hospital ourselves for minor things: I had wisdom teeth extracted, and Peter had a dislocated elbow reset. Kara had been in hospital a few months earlier for her vesicoureteral reflux (urine flowing backwards from the bladder to the kidneys). She had surgery because she was at risk for kidney infections or other damage. We were upset that Kara required surgery, which we considered serious. We had spent eight days in hospital with her, but there weren't many big machines pinging and beeping, like all the equipment that accompanies heart surgery. The day of procedures was huge for us. Peter and I were solely focused on Avelynn and not on what was happening around us. We had tunnel vision, and everyone wanted to test and prod our precious baby.

To ensure there were no surprises during her surgery, Avelynn had an "echo" (echocardiogram—an ultrasound that can look into the heart to see how it is functioning) and an ECG (electrocardiogram—which measures and records the electrical activity of the heart). Avelynn previously had both procedures in Perth, but that wasn't sufficient; doctors at the Royal Children's Hospital were very thorough. The doctors told us Avelynn had a very strong heart. It proved to be amazingly strong during that first week in the ICU.

It was awful holding Avelynn down for blood tests with syringes that were almost as big as her forearm and needles that looked as large as her fingers. They put a tight tourniquet on her forearm to bring her veins up so the doctor could get a blood sample. Avelynn screamed and started turning a motley blue, which freaked me out, because I knew she wasn't breathing properly. Avelynn didn't seem grateful to the medical team who were trying to help her, but I appreciated their efforts and thanked them.

We had a sober conversation with Avelynn's surgeon and also asked the anaesthetist some pretty serious questions. Both said she should be okay, and faced a maximum of ten days in hospital. They also warned us that a truncus repair can be a bit tricky. Truncus babies can develop high blood pressure in their lungs even after surgery, although it usually self-corrects.

I heard lots of medical jargon that we really didn't understand, and felt that we needed a medical dictionary. We asked the doctors to write down what they were talking about, and we still do. We believed that we had a right to know the worst case scenario; but understandably, most people probably don't. Peter especially asked many questions about Avelynn's risks; his motto is, "always know what's around the corner."

We knew nothing about this type of procedure and weren't yet connected to the Internet. Our kids were young and we were unaware that we could have all the world's knowledge at our fingertips. Before Avelynn's surgery, we were scared of talking frankly to the specialists and we were uncertain of the correct protocol. It seemed surreal to drink coffee while we chatted with the anaesthetist about the risks of Avelynn's heart surgery.

He told us the worst that could happen, "She could have a cerebral haemorrhage," also known as a "stroke," which meant Avelynn could have a bleed in her brain. Before that conversation, we had no idea that children could have strokes during or after heart surgery. The thought of that happening to our precious, dear baby was not welcome; we put it to the back of our minds and tried not to concentrate on the worst outcome.

The little-known and unwelcome truth is that, in Australia, congenital and acquired heart disease are the number one killers of children under the age of eleven. We certainly didn't know that before we were introduced to the world of heart kids. Everyone seems aware of the dangers of children drowning, being killed in household accidents, cot deaths, and automobile accidents.

Parents are told not to leave nappy buckets full of water on the floor, and there are strict rules in Australia on pool fences. There are all sorts of safety measures that we learn as parents and that we teach our kids, but how many parents know anything about heart disease in children? It seems to be a secret. Sure, it's confronting, but no one seems to think it will happen to him; just as Peter and I didn't. I can tell you: *nothing* prepares you for having a child with heart disease.

No matter how hard it is for me to talk about Avelynn in this way, the main reason for writing this book is to share this information with other parents. Peter and I didn't plan on having a kid with any problems, certainly not one with heart disease. We only hope Avelynn's story will inspire people with her strength and realise that sometimes children can take a lot of knocks and still bounce back.

It sometimes seems that we are unable to protect our children from harm, although we so desperately want to. We have in-built instincts to protect our kids at any cost; to jump in the way of an oncoming car if necessary. The reality of having Avelynn is that she had to go through massive invasive open-heart surgery in order to save her life. No matter how anyone tried to assure me otherwise, I felt like a horrible parent, as though I had somehow put her in this predicament

Late that afternoon, after all of Avelynn's procedures, we were very subdued as we returned to our hotel. No words can fully describe how unbearable the night before surgery was. Avelynn was lying in between us, but we did not sleep that night for fear of what the next day might bring. Avelynn knew we were there for her, and we told her how much we loved her. Peter and I looked into each other's eyes, and we knew we couldn't speak our biggest fear: losing her. Even the *thought* of losing a child is so traumatic, you want to reject the possibility as soon as it occurs.

As I lay in bed, I couldn't help but think about life and how we had arrived at this point. I reflected upon a couple of very chilling dreams, one that occurred only a couple of weeks previously and the other in 1996, when two Black Hawk helicopters collided during a night manoeuvre.

Chapter 14

My Dreams

I have a heightened sense of intuition—what some might call psychic abilities. Don't get me wrong, I'm not clairvoyant. I don't know the future, so don't ask. It seems to be some type of sixth sense, but who knows?

The Black Hawk tragedy in 1996, which cost the lives of fifteen SASR and three Aviation Regiment men, was Australia's worst peacetime military disaster. The night before that accident, I had a very scary dream, a nightmare from which I couldn't escape. In my dream, I could see through the cockpit of the helicopter into the small, dark, tight space, to the SAS men wearing night vision goggles.

I saw one of Peter's mates was among the SAS guys, so I knew they were on the helicopter; though I knew instinctively it wasn't actually him. I don't know how I knew that, but he was representing the SASR guys for me. Another weird detail: I somehow knew Peter's two best mates weren't on the helicopter, even though Peter told me the next day they would have been.

What I saw chilled me to the bone, and still gives me the creeps. I dreamed the SAS guys were falling in the helicopter, on-fire and dying, but they were not panicking. It was so bloody awful, calling it a nightmare doesn't come close. My dream kept recurring, and I couldn't sleep well. I hit Peter across the head a few times and he turned to me and said, "Hey what have I done? What, Michelle?" But I didn't fully wake.

I continued to toss and turn, and Peter told me my sobbing woke him. It was awful! I dreamt they were falling through space with masks on their faces, but I didn't know what the masks were until morning. When I described them to Peter, he told me they were night vision goggles, which I had never seen before.

The guys were falling through space and were trying to hang on. I was reaching out to them in my dream; I knew they were dying, but there was nothing I could do. In the morning, Peter asked me why I had hit him and carried on so much, and I told him about my dream. He said, "What the hell are you talking about, Michelle?" I yelled back at him, "I want to know if you guys are flying on planes or helicopters. What's going on, Peter? What are you guys up to, because I had this nightmare where guys were killed?"

Peter couldn't tell me, which really pissed me off. Even though I knew he wasn't supposed to tell me, I thought he might because I was so upset. So I shut-up, and pondered my nightmare. Peter went to work as usual, but later that day we heard the tragic news: two helicopters had collided, and eighteen guys had been killed. We didn't know, however who was, or wasn't, accounted for; it was tragic. Peter had thought two of his best mates were on the helicopters, but I was certain that they weren't.

Peter and I couldn't be by ourselves, so we went next door to our neighbours, who were also crying and in shock. We hung onto each other for support while waiting for more news. We thanked God it wasn't our husbands and that they were by our sides. For the life of us, we couldn't imagine what the women whose husbands had been killed were doing, but our hearts went out to them.

Much later I took Peter home and cuddled him to me, as I had Ayla when she was a baby. I tried to comfort and reassure him. I kept telling him I knew his mates were not on the helicopter. He would not believe me and eventually fell into an exhausted sleep. What spun me out was that the accident happened exactly as I had dreamt it, even down to the night vision goggles. One thing stands out in my mind is that I sensed no fear when I saw the flames and felt them falling. They were brave to the very end.

The other dream I had was about Avelynn and her brush with death, or that's how I interpreted it. In this dream, there was a deep hole in the ground—totally black. A male figure was down in the hole, beckoning to me with his hands to come and join him. I knew he represented death and he wanted me to come down into the whole with him and bring Avelynn. In my dream, I had to sit down at the edge of the hole; I didn't want to, I was compelled to. I had to sit at the hole, mesmerised by the figure beckoning me with his hands. He had such an assurance about him that I had to obey; it was really scary stuff.

He was commanding me to jump, although I tried to resist, I couldn't. As I slid closer to the edge about to drop down to him, he suddenly raised his hand to prevent me from jumping. At the last second, a tiny bit of white light shone, so I wasn't allowed to jump down to him. The light represented life, so I wasn't allowed to jump down into the hole. Death stopped waving to me and let me go. It wasn't that clear-cut or unemotional; I had felt utter, mind-numbing fear that took my breath away. I awoke, unable to breathe. I cried and tossed from side to side, unable to sleep. It had seemed so real.

This dream was about a week before Avelynn's surgery and left me extremely fearful that Avelynn would have a brush with death.

Chapter 15

Wonderful Cardiologists: Holding My Heart in Your Hand

The memories of my dream about Avelynn stayed with me the night before her surgery as I held her to me, trying not to disturb her. Peter was sound asleep, and I cherished this precious time with her. I forced myself to think positively; I kept telling myself that her surgery and hospital stay would be alright.

I had just gone to sleep when we received a phone call telling us that surgery was definitely on and to bring Avelynn by seven in the morning. One of the hardest things as a mum was not feed her, as Avelynn was fasting. I felt like the worst mother and asked Peter to hold her, since he did not smell of breast milk. She quieted down for a little while. Once at the hospital, we made our way to pre-surgery where we waited with other parents and their children who were also having surgery that day.

We didn't have long to wait; Avelynn would require all day, so she was first on the list. Unfortunately, only one parent was allowed to accompany each child to the operating theatre and that was me. I felt sorry for Peter, but I was desperate to be with her for the few moments before I handed her over to the surgical team. Peter gave her a fierce hug and tried to be brave, but I saw the tears in his eyes.

Peter knew I had to be there, not him; I was breast feeding and my hormones were raging. As people say, don't come between a lioness and her cub. I knew Peter wished he could come with me and Avelynn, but he was fantastic and understood that it had to be me. My heart went out to Peter not being there in her last moments before the heart surgery.

As I followed one of the green penguins—my nickname for the surgical team members, who were all dressed in green from head to over-sized shoe covers—I tried to keep my emotions in check, if not for my sake then for Avelynn's. Those feelings threatened to overwhelm me, but I didn't want her to sense my sadness for fear of upsetting her.

I wasn't allowed to hold her when they gave her the general anaesthetic, but I gave her the best mum-cuddles and kisses she'd ever received. I tried to give her my strength, love, and support while imprinting her face and body into my memory in case it was the last time I ever saw her. My dream somehow gave me strength; it represented a brush with death, but life had won in the end.

My mother-hormones were raging and urging me to run like a tigress and claw the surgeon from head to toe to get my baby back. I was trying to override protective instincts not to let her have the surgery that might cost her life. But I knew I had no choice; without the surgery she would die of heart failure within a few months. Such is the nature of her congenital heart defect.

Walking back to Peter empty handed, knowing I wouldn't see our baby for as long as eight or nine hour,s left me numb and speechless. Peter walked up and gave me the biggest cuddle, no words were necessary. Having our child go through major heart surgery is not something we ever thought we'd have to experience. How does one prepare emotionally? It was hard enough preparing for my third child within five years without this extra load.

I knew I could prepare physically and organise my household. Making arrangements for Ayla and Kara,; making sure I had their favourite toys and special cuddling teddy bears, organising time off from school for Ayla, and cancelling Kara's child care. Organising a neighbour to feed our dog, ensuring the cats were booked into their wonderful cattery, and ensuring we all had enough clothes for our time in Melbourne when we left Perth. All of that was easy. But preparing yourself for your baby's heart surgery was not in any parenting manual that I had ever found. I was terrified of Avelynn's surgery; I couldn't face losing her.

Statistically, there was a five percent chance that Avelynn could die under the knife. So I was tried to concentrate on the ninety-five percent probability that she would be okay. Sometimes, I couldn't keep the monsters away from my thoughts, and I became quite negative about my life and how the surgery might turn out. Most of the time I coped okay, just concentrated on being grateful for what I did have in my life.

I had gone out of my way to ensure Avelynn's first experiences in life were wonderful and always said to myself that if anything went wrong then at least Avelynn had the best nine weeks any baby could ask for. But preparing yourself mentally for the unknown is hard. No one I had spoken to really wanted to talk about having a baby go through open-heart surgery, or how they managed emotionally when things went wrong. In essence, I didn't have anything to which I could refer to guide me along the way.

I'd asked a couple of other heart kids parents over the phone how their child went with the truncus repair, and they told me, "Yes, it's stressful but the surgeons are fantastic!" "Avelynn will be fine, she's in the best place." "Stay positive, it will all work out." "Go somewhere! Get out of the hospital and get your mind off the surgery." No one told me, "You'll be so stressed, you could chew your way through a large bone," which is exactly how I felt

The essence of having another baby was to bring joy into our house through another child for us and a sibling for Ayla and Kara. Not fear, worry, stress, and the thought of her undergoing open-heart surgery. I knew I wasn't prepared mentally for the challenges which I knew we would have to face, but I also knew we had to face them as surely as I had given birth to Avelynn.

I knew it was my fundamental nature to cope—I had already been through so much—and going through adversity brings out your core strength, what you are really made of. It brings out the skills we have devised and built over a lifetime of tests and challenges to all of life's experiences—good and bad. But I knew my coping skills in the end would be tested in the extreme; I knew

I'd learn what I was made of, and that even if the challenges grew too great, I couldn't run away.

Peter and I haven't really spoken to anyone about our innermost feelings and what we went through during Avelynn's heart surgery, the ICU, and our entire hospital stay. I've kept too much inside. I hadn't delved into my feelings too much as I am sure I would have scared people off. It's not that I haven't tried, but the person I'm speaking with usually starts getting fidgety, looks away, and generally doesn't know what to say.

Often people tell me, "Well modern medicine is great," or ask, "How can babies die of heart disease?" "It can't be that bad, it's not like she's got cancer." Some make other remarks that don't help, but which I know they are well meant.

Fortunately I have found great support amongst other "Heart Kid" families and know from experience it's just too darn confronting for most people. I suppose the thought of a child going through a major heart operation that's life threatening can be confronting to some people. There's a lack of understanding in the general community about just how many babies and children go through heart surgery. Twice as many children die from heart disease than cancer in Australia.

I am in not implying either is better, both are awful. The worst thing that can happen is for your child to die, no matter the cause. I also have to remember how ignorant I was of children's heart disease before I had Avelynn. I thought the worst that could happen was a baby born with a hole in its heart, like my friend in high school, and she was fine.

One of my aims is to raise awareness of congenital heart disease (children are born with it) and acquired heart disease (children are infected with rheumatic fever, other bacteria, or another infection).

But I hope that if you're reading this book you may be more interested than most. At times what I've written, may be confronting, but at least through reading this, you'll have a greater understanding of what heart kids and their families experience. I hope to taking some of the fear out of the equation. I know that people are scared for their children. Parents of a heart kid, or of a child who's given their parents and doctors a scare, must face their child's and their own mortality.

This is the reason—or one of them— why I am sure heart kids are just so confronting. Many of us have had to face the fact that our child might not come home, and those life and death situations make you wonder about the meaning of life.

I don't hold back in this book so be warned. I've sometimes been called too honest; I call a spade a spade and this is a firsthand experience of what it's like to go through our child's heart surgery. From reading many other parents' stories about their heart kids, we know there are a lot of similarities.

What we felt probably applies to a lot of other major surgeries, child or adult. We each deal with surgery in our individual ways As with Avelynn's truncus repair, you have to weigh the risks and benefits and hope at the end of the day, that you've made the right choice. The ultimate aim is improving the child's or adult's life.

After I handed Avelynn over to the surgeon and walked back to Peter we settled in for the long wait. Waiting during the hours of Avelynn's heart surgery was incredibly hard, one of the hardest periods I've ever had to endure. The uncertainty and the unfamiliar feeling of not being in control nearly suffocated us that day.

Thank goodness, mum had taken Ayla and Kara to the zoo. We couldn't focus on them, we couldn't even think of each other, we could only focus on our fear of the operation and what the outcome meant to the future of our family. Maybe it was the loss of control, but I felt completely useless. As a mum, I felt like I needed to help Avelynn, to do something constructive, but there was nothing.

It was totally up to the surgeons and their skill; I kept reminding myself that the Royal Children's Hospital in Melbourne has a fantastic, first-class cardiac team, including a fabulous ICU with wonderful staff who really know their stuff. Each year, the RCH cardiac team performs 400-to-500 operations on babies and children's hearts requiring cardiopulmonary bypass. They were the best in all of Australasia, and possibly the world.

I had absolute confidence in the skill of the surgeons and knew that Avelynn was in the best place for her cardiac surgery. It's not just the surgeon operating on her but a whole team, including pulmonary experts on the bypass machine and experienced doctors and nurses in the ICU. They come not just from Australia but from all over the world to gain valuable experience and give us valuable knowledge in return.

We had flown to Melbourne, because in 1999, Perth simply didn't have the facilities or the staff to perform Avelynn's type of heart surgery. Avelynn's surgeon is French, and he's fantastic; I am so glad he's in Melbourne. I have spoken to him about the wonderful job he does, and he said it's his job, and although I know it requires immense patience, dedication, and skill, he considers it all in a day's work. For us parents it's more than that; it's a chance for our children with heart problems to experience a normal life. It's a chance for their siblings to take them home from hospital and grow up together. I feel I can never repay my debt of gratitude to the surgeon and the entire cardiac team.

I kept telling myself that Avelynn was the lucky one, although it upsets me to remember all the babies and children who must go through this. They are fortunate to live in Australia. The unlucky children who live in third world countries often don't get the chance to see a cardiologist or receive the required surgery. It is a matter of survival; without the surgeon's skill, Avelynn would not be here.

Thinking about the surgeon's skill was one thing but applying it to what was being done to Avelynn was another. Our information came from the cardiac team in Perth and from answers to the questions we bombarded the surgeon with during our brief meeting after we arrived in Melbourne.

My only other experience with heart surgery was of my grandfather, who underwent a quadruple bypass when I was sixteen years old. My family told me basically nothing about what happened. It was not an exaggeration to say we were complete novices. It was comforting that her surgeon was very confident and said Avelynn's health was fantastic, including her weight, which we had worked so hard to achieve.

When we asked about possible complications, we weren't told much and understood less. I imagined the surgeon did not really want to contemplate the negative. We had a rough idea she'd be put onto a bypass machine, how he was going to repair her heart, and that was pretty much it. I suppose Peter and I didn't like to dwell on the negatives either and didn't ask enough questions.

Just the thought of our precious girl being cut open and having her tiny heart operated on was too real in itself without knowing all the gruesome details. I really couldn't go there, it was in the "too hard" basket and unlike the surgeon, I was emotionally involved in her surgery. Plus, I had to contend with my haunting dream that warned of unforeseen fears. I only wanted to hold the vision of a happy child in my mind's eye, not see her knocked out cold on the table.

It was years later that I could bring myself to finally look up on the World Wide Web and understand things like the bypass machine and what her surgery involved. I'll discuss it here, so if you don't want to know then don't read the next page.

Cardiopulmonary bypass is when your child is connected to a Heart-Lung Machine (HLM), which is required for open-heart surgery. The heart needs to be empty and in most cases needs to be stopped for a while. During that time, no blood flows through the heart and lungs; the HLM does the work of both so the surgeon can operate on the still heart. The HLM pumps blood through the body, adds oxygen to the blood, removes carbon dioxide, and controls the body's temperature.

The HLM has a series of individual microprocessor units that monitor and control patient temperature, blood gases, and safety systems. The patient is connected to the circuit through plastic cannulae, which the surgeon inserts into a large vein and an artery at the beginning of surgery and removes at the end.

The first thing the cardiac team do is fill the tubing circuit with a special priming solution, a mixture of donor blood and saline solution. The priming solution removes all the air in the circuit, oxygenator, and filter and makes it bubble free. The donor blood, usually about 500 millilitres, is necessary to prime the tubing circuit because children who weigh less than sixteen kilogrammes don't have a enough of their own blood to fill the HLM.

During cardiopulmonary bypass, the patient's temperature must be controlled. During most cardiac operations patients are cooled in order to slow their oxygen use. The level of cooling is determined by the type of operation, and the body temperature is controlled by altering the blood temperature in the oxygenator. The patient is warmed back up to normal body temperature towards the end of cardiopulmonary bypass.

The perfusionist is the member of the team responsible for the operation of the HLM. The perfusionist is also responsible for the selection and set-up of the circuit components for the procedure. The perfusionist works closely with the surgeon and anaesthetist, and is a skilled scientist with tertiary qualification including human physiology and biochemistry, as well as specialised training in the techniques of artificial blood circulation.

When the surgeon has finished the repair, and the team feels that the heart and lungs can take over from the HLM, the perfusionist slowly weans the patient and the surgeon removes the cannula. Visit www.rch.org.au/cardiac_surgery/perfusion for more information

Thinking of our beautiful baby girl, who we'd only had nine short weeks, being operated on was not a place our minds wanted to be. What do they say, "Ignorance is bliss?" I don't know about the bliss bit, but the ignorance bit sure helped. The hours slowly ticked by, although time ceased to have any meaning for us and appeared to stop.

After a while, we realised it was lunch time. We weren't hungry, but decided we should eat something from the hospital cafe. The coffee was great, and went down a treat. We had a couple of people visit us, which helped regulate our day; my younger cousin came and I remember just looking at him, especially at his eyebrow. He'd had it pierced, and I was fascinated. It worked a treat as a distraction and gave us something to talk about. I stirred him up about it as we tried to lighten the mood and avoid dwelling on Avelynn's surgery.

Mum and the girls came back from the zoo around four. They'd enjoyed their day out and wanted to know where their baby was and if they could see her. Mum had fully expected us to be in the ICU with Avelynn by then and said, "Hey Michelle! What's going on? Why are you still out here in the cafe? What's the story with Avelynn?" I said, "Listen, mum, they won't tell us anything.

They won't let us into the ICU to see her, even though we know she's in there." Mum said, "Why don't you go with Peter while I look after the girls again? Go and see what's going on, okay? Just go and try to find out something." "Come on, Peter. Let's go," I said. Five minutes later we were back with mum and the girls in the cafe. I was crying and knew something was going on. "They still won't let us in, mum! I don't know what to do! We still don't know what's happening." Sitting with my head in my hands, I felt completely lost. I wanted to know what the hell was going on!

About half an hour later, a nurse we knew happened into the cafe. Peter and I were really concerned that something terrible had happened to Avelynn. We walked up, grabbed her, and demanded she tell us if she knew anything. "Well, Avelynn's in the ICU. Haven't they told you anything?" "No, they haven't. We just want to know what's going on."

As we high-tailed it out of the cafe, we were grateful to the nurse for showing us the way to the ICU. We had forgotten where it was and would have probably lost our way walking around the hospital. I'm sure the nurse was on her dinner break, but she was so kind and helpful.

The cardiac team is now much better at keeping parents informed of what's happening. They realise it can cause massive anxiety for the parents not to know what's going on and that you want to be kept informed of your child's progress, even if they've still got a couple of hours to go. It's information you need to know. Then you can think, "Well, okay. Now I know I can drink my coffee and possibly eat something so I don't fall over. When you hadn't eaten anything all day, your head starts to feel detached and floating from low blood sugar and stress. Not a great combination on top of too much coffee or tea, or the amount of chocolate one can somehow consume.

With much trepidation, Peter and I stood at the locked doors of the ICU and buzzed, waiting impatiently for an answer over the intercom. Peter said, "Yes, hi! We're Avelynn Woods parents, and we want to come in and see her now!" He must have sounded pretty assertive, and they finally let us through. We still knew nothing of Avelynn's condition since a brief chat to her surgeon hours ago, simply telling us that he had finished and the surgery had gone well. Little did we know what was in store for us behind those locked doors!

Chapter 16

The ICU—Behind Closed Doors

Just inside the ICU, on the left-hand side, there was a basin with a sign reminding visitors to wash their hands. A poster of how to expertly clean with the disinfectant supplied reminded visitors again that germs weren't welcome. I scrubbed my hands diligently, hopeful that I'd removed all traces of the nasty bacteria. There was a small medical-equipment storage room across from the basin, adjacent to two intensive care rooms, each fitted with three patient beds. A bit farther along was two-patient room that could be opened to an adjacent room that could accommodate three or four additional patients.

The hub, the brain, the control centre of the ICU was a computer area opposite the last room on the right side of the hall. Nurses, doctors, and clerks worked seriously in front of computers; their whispered discussions occasionally interrupted by quiet laughter, which did not seem to fit the sombre atmosphere. But who am I to say? Perhaps it was funny.

There was a sign beside the bench in the computer area, "Chocolates for Sale—Please Support the ICU." "Hmmm, chocolates and stress," I thought, "They'll get my support." Posters depicted stories of fragile babies and children, most with the theme, "How the ICU saved my child." Sadly, sometimes not, but the stories praised the dedicated staff anyway.

The ambience was sombre. I was unaccustomed to the sights, smells, and sounds of the of the ICU as I walked past the computer hub on my left side. Each of the five rooms could accommodate four-to -six patients. Most of the rooms have a pleasant outside view and all are well equipped, with bedside monitoring and other equipment used to care for critically ill babies and children.

Each room has its own telephone, so relatives and parents can receive phone calls without leaving their children. The ICU is close to the operating suite, radiology, laboratory, and the hospital's helipad. The ICU also provides a service called Medical Emergency Team (MET) to the rest of the hospital; MET respond to emergencies in the wards, the hospital lobby, and occasionally even at the McDonald's® restaurant downstairs.

I followed the nurse to the entrance of two large rectangular rooms separated by a wall but with large, open doorways. As we approached the large room, we passed a trolley filled with every imaginable medical necessity: bandages, band aids, catheters, syringes, swabs, drugs, bottles, syringes, and many that I didn't recognise. But I wasn't really paying much attention; I was on high alert, looking my baby.

The ICU at the Royal Children's Hospital admits children who require care and treatment not available in the general wards. Care is provided by a team including a duty consultant, experienced doctors (called "registrars"), nurses, and technologists. It has eighteen beds and primarily services the states of Victoria and New South Wales, but admits children from all of Australia. The ICU treats about 1,300 children annually, including those with heart disease, major trauma, severe respiratory disease, multi-organ failure, haematologic, and oncological diseases.

Avelynn was one of the 500-to-600 children operated on for heart disease each year. But we weren't really prepared.

> **Avelynn's operation started at eight in the morning and lasted nine hours. This was a long stressful wait. It's a massive shock seeing her in the ICU because her chest is still open; they can't close it due to the pressure of her pulmonary arteries. I held her hand and placed my other one on the top of her head. She's heavily sedated, and I'm in shock. I feel heavy, a little teary, and my heart aches like a weight is attached to it. Avelynn's condition is very critical and unstable with her pressures fluctuating wildly. She's fighting and so are the medical team. She's on ten drugs, and connected to seventeen tubes and wires. I can literately see her heart beat-**

> **ing. The girls stayed at mums. Ayla and Kara did not see their sister today. That was just as well because it would be too hard for them. Kara had already asked this morning, over the phone "Where are they taking my baby?"**
>
> **My diary, Tuesday, 16 November 1999**

The nurse pointed to Avelynn in her ICU bed. It was a tiny cot, not very deep, with glass sides to stop her from rolling out. The cot had an L-shaped heating lamp for extra warmth when needed. I was aware of other children in the room, but paid no attention to them.

We walked tentatively to her. I was holding my breath in trepidation, ordering myself to keep calm, not knowing what I would see, or how I would respond. After the surgeon told us (only hours ago—but it seemed another day) that her operation was success, we'd been told nothing more.

Before Avelynn's surgery, Peter and I had refused a tour of the ICU because we didn't want to be confronted with anyone else's sick child, especially a baby. We thought at the time that we were pretty tough; both of us had seen dead bodies before, and thought we were somewhat hardened to life's unpleasantries. "Hey," I thought optimistically, "how bad can it be?" We were not prepared to see Avelynn with her chest open. Perhaps nothing could have prepared us for that; it was such a shock. I nearly passed out. I used to be a veterinary nurse and have seen a lot of gruesome surgery, but seeing Avelynn, lying there with her chest open was something different.

I didn't know what to do. I was highly emotional. Wow! I didn't realise children could be left with their chests open after surgery. It was something I wasn't prepared for. I never expected to see her heart!

This scenario was never been explained to Peter or me. Because it was unexpected, I felt afraid, helpless, and confused. I had no time to prepare for the stress of seeing her in this critical state. I stared at her beating heart, completely transfixed.

My brain was trying to make sense of a picture that it could hardly comprehend. It seemed so unreal. I could see Avelynn's heart beating. Staring at her tiny, delicate heart made me more conscious of what difficult surgery she underwent and the incredible skill of her wonderful surgeon. It's hard to imagine having the patience and dexterity to operate and repair a defect inside of a baby's heart.

Incredible and fascinating as it was, I thought, "If I don't leave now, or get a grip on myself, I am going to pass out, and that won't help." But I nearly didn't make it; I was mesmerized by her beating heart. Within moments the world started to go black; I saw stars swimming before my eyes, and I felt a roaring pressure in my head, as if I'd been hanging upside down too long on the monkey bars.

As my vision blurred, I thought, "Hey, wow! I am about to pass out," but I got control of my legs and somehow made it out of there without collapsing. I told myself, "Okay I've seen her now. Wow, that was tough. I don't know how I'm going to manage seeing her again, but I must." I was shaking and not quite in control of myself.

Peter and I held and supported each other on the way out of the room. "Oh! My God, Peter, did you see her heart? I can't believe they didn't have it covered! Why didn't they tell us?" Tears were streaming down my face, and I could hardly talk. Peter looked like a stunned mullet and couldn't say much either. We were standing in the parents' lounge within the ICU. Neither of us knew what was going on or what we could do. Both of us were terrified, but we didn't know why. Maybe it was the shock of seeing her so exposed, her heart so vulnerable. She looked so delicate, and we felt helpless.

Although I felt awful, I was reluctant to be away from her and said to Peter, "We'd better go back in now; maybe it won't be so bad this time." Peter had this far away look in his eyes and simply nodded. We knew it would be a hard thing to do, but we didn't want to leave Avelynn for long.

Only five minutes had elapsed from the time we walked out of her room until we went back to see her. I'd gotten my breathing under control, and although I still felt shaky, my dizziness had gone and my head felt clearer.

Seeing Avelynn again, I wasn't prepared for another shock: she looked even worse. I could hardly believe it; condensation had formed underneath the plastic covering that they had put over her heart. Just when I thought I'd seen enough, and had told myself to be tough, I had to come to grips with that gruesome plastic covering. I really don't know what it was; it looked like a plastic membrane protecting Avelynn's heart from infection. The plastic totally enclosed her chest, like Glad® wrap.

Watching her little heart beating away beneath the plastic freaked me out; or maybe it was the condensation, which reminded me of water dripping down the window pane on a cold day. Seeing condensation under the plastic just seemed improbable, and I was trying to keep a grip on reality. I wondered how many more shocks I could endure, as this one really took the cake. But true to form, I rapidly adjusted and grew used to seeing Avelynn's heart through the gap in her chest. I started to believe that, possibly, I could cope, but I was scared of what it all meant.

It seemed incredible that her tiny heart was the cause of so much fuss; it was beautiful and looked blameless. Though in those first ten minutes or so, I didn't comprehend how fragile her heart really was, as it innocently beat away. That I could see her heart was a surreal and unnatural experience; something I never expected or imagined.

I wondered how the hell I was supposed to protect her now. I was frightened and stressed; helpless to comfort her when she needed me most. Eventually, I recovered from the shock of seeing her heart beating underneath the plastic covering and slowly became aware of my surroundings. I started taking in what was happening around me.

Avelynn had her own trolley from which the nurses worked. It was full of syringes, needles, tape, labels, and a yellow sharps container for disposing of used needles. A yellow infectious waste bin was hanging off the side of the trolley. One of the trolley drawer held drugs prescribed for Avelynn. Her cot had its own light and heater. The fluorescent lights in the ceiling would be dimmed at night.

My neck prickled with unease as people rushed around Avelynn. "Oh, my God! Oh, my God," I thought, "What's going on?" Six or seven nurses and doctors were working on her. It was a scene from "Emergency" and we were spectators, except this wasn't a movie set. It was our daughter they were saving.

I wanted to know what medications they were giving her. They were pumping a mixture of drugs into her and I asked one of the nurses, "Why do you keep giving her those drugs?" She answered curtly, as finally dawned on me: they were trying to save Avelynn's life.

Perhaps this should have been obvious but we hadn't been told anything, or been briefed on Avelynn's condition. I guessed the ICU staff thought we knew what was going on and giving us a rundown of her condition wasn't their first priority.

Neither Peter nor I had previously set foot in an ICU. This was our first experience of dealing with such an emergency, and we didn't comprehend what was unfolding. At first, we really didn't understand that they were saving her life or how hard Avelynn was fighting. Would it have made any difference if we had known? I'm not sure.

Later, when it dawned on me that they had been saving her life, I felt incredibly stupid not to realize that her condition was critical. We had nothing with which to compare what we saw. We never know what normal was in an ICU, or how many nurses and doctors look after one child, how often she was given drugs, or why and when the machines connected to the patient buzz and beep. We had no basis for comparison; for all we knew, it was normal for all of those serious-looking people to rush around her.

I felt stupid initially, but I suppose Peter and I shouldn't have felt too bad, as we had to guess that her situation was critical. No one had said, "Hey, Michelle and Peter! Your child is fighting for her life—stand back while we do our best to save her!" No, we had to guess, and then to cope without understanding what was going on, without assurance that "everything will be okay!"

No one spoke directly to us during that initial stage, which lasted half an hour or so. We were front-row spectators, without knowing what to do, or what was expected of us.

Peter was overwhelmed. He went back to the cafe and told my mum what was going on and said good-bye to Ayla and Kara. When I came back, he told me the girls were staying with mum. We thought it best they didn't see Avelynn just yet; we could hardly contain our grief and could not have answered the girls' questions.

Avelynn had stiff boards and intravenous (IV) lines attached to both arms. The boards were to prevent her from moving her arms, although she was also heavily sedated. Monitors and more IVs were attached. She had a urinary catheter, a nasal gastric tube up her nose and down to her stomach, and a ventilator tube in her trachea (windpipe). The ventilator forced breathable air into Avelynn's lungs through an endotracheal tube to give her heart and lungs a chance to rest. It was hard to find a spot on Avelynn's body that didn't have a tube or wire attached. We tried to touch her fingers, but even they were wrapped in crepe bandages, securing the boards to her arms.

Two nurses continued to work with Avelynn, and it all got the better of me; I just had to know what was happening. Once the situation seemed a bit under control, I started asking a lot of questions, desperately trying to educate myself.

I asked, "What's in the IVs?" "What do the different coloured lines on the monitor mean?" "What do the abbreviations on the monitors mean?" "Why do you inject her with drugs so often?" "Is she going to be okay? "When will you know?" "Why is she having so much trouble?" "What do you mean, 'Her pressures are all over the place?'" Mostly I just muttered to myself, "Oh, my God," as I watched and waited.

The nurses and doctor were working quickly the whole time, trying to keep her stable. We later learned that Avelynn's pulmonary artery (PA) pressures were too high, and the staff were trying frantically trying to lower the pressure to stabilize her. We were told she was on drugs that paralysed her body so she couldn't even twitch. She had morphine for pain, and various other drugs.

Reluctantly, I had to leave Avelynn's side for half an hour. My breasts were so engorged that I had to find a room to express my milk and then find bottles and tags. Basically, to become familiar with the breast milk expressing system, to learn out how to label the milk I'd expressed for Avelynn, and where I could safely store it. This time I was positive. I thought it's the least I can do for my little bubby; I was sure she'd soon need it.

The situation in the ICU when I returned was much the same as when I'd left and continued in the same vein for a several hours. We were asked to leave about eleven that night. They were struggling to keep her alive and promised to ring if anything happened over night. With all my heart, I wanted to stay by her side in case she needed me, to nurture and protect her. She seemed so fragile, but I couldn't pick her up. I wanted to give Avelynn my strength, to somehow inject it into her, or take her place if I could.

Peter wished he could take Avelynn's place. He wanted to take away her pain, and would have literally given her his heart. I was glad the nurses didn't hear that he wanted to die if that would have saved his baby. I started again to feel overwhelmed, not knowing what would happen with Avelynn. Peter scared the hell out of me talking crazy like that. We only knew that Avelynn was fighting a massive battle for her life, and she had to win. We had to hope, beyond all reason, that Ave would be okay. Earlier in the day, we'd checked into the parents' accommodation at the hospital. With heavy hearts, we made our way there while we tried to take it all in.

Avelynn's whole situation was overwhelming. Peter and I cried so much; my eyes were swollen, and my nose was blocked. My heart felt like it would burst. I kept crying, I was overwhelmed and I couldn't go on. No amount of self-talk could console me. "Come on, Michelle! Everything will be alright." "How could Avelynn die?" "Babies don't die, do they?" "We make em tough; how could anything happen to her?" Peter and I had no words for each other; we were so weighed down by raw pain and emotion, we did not know how to speak.

There were no promises. The road looked bleak, and the tears flowed. We felt miserable. I wondered how we could function and care for ourselves, let alone our other two children. The girls would be coming tomorrow to see their baby sister, expecting to hold her, to play protective mothers to her. How the hell were we going to face them and tell them that their baby might die? Worse, what if she died overnight?

I'd never felt more hopeless or useless. My heart had crumbled into tiny pieces, and I wondered how or if I could put it back together. I put the covers over my head and held Peter's hand, crying and crying as I hadn't done since I was a child. Eventually I fell asleep of sheer exhaustion, and slept until six.

> **My big day. I had a long day, and mum and dad must be worried. Now I know when they mean by an operating theatre. The surgeons, doctors, nurses, and perfusionist are covered in green, with gloves and funny lights. After that, I went to the ICU. Aren't they noisy? I am not out of the woods yet; I need a lot of support. Worse still, they have to cool me down to thirty-five degrees Celsius, I'm on a muscle relaxant, and my chest is not properly closed.**
>
> **Avelynn's diary, Tuesday, 16 November 1999**

Chapter 17

In the ICU—Fighting for Breath

Avelynn is more stable; pressures seem okay. I walked to the Royal Women's Hospital, about two kilometres away, and had physio at half-past two for my coccyx broken giving birth to Avelynn. Peter and I went to shops and bought food supplies. We can't think very well, working on automatic. Girls at mums tonight so we ate take-a-way. Yuck, I'm getting sick of it already.

Avelynn more stable because they put her on an ice-pad and got her body temperature down to thirty-two or thrity-three degrees Celsius. She's cold to touch, but it seems to be working.

My diary, Wednesday, 17 November 1999

Upon awakening the morning after Avelynn's heart surgery I stopped crying—just like that. We had a long hard road ahead of us. Avelynn's fight wasn't over, not by a long shot. I knew, I didn't want to admit it to myself yet. Furthermore, it's as though my body decided that crying took too much energy; that I had to conserve what strength I had just to keep going.

To could keep going, Peter and I stopped thinking about life before Avelynn's heart surgery; before she was in this critical situation; before all the "what ifs…?" We stopped projecting about any future life with her at home. We couldn't think about the future with Avelynn, because we didn't know if she had a future.

As sad as it may seem, we felt it would be tempting fate to think about life after the hospital. We were afraid, somehow, that any positive thoughts of bringing her home and watching her grow would jeopardise her chances. Our brains couldn't go to those areas where dark and painful thoughts lie in wait ready to mock us. The thought of not bringing her home was unbearable.

If we allowed ourselves to fantasize about bringing home a healthy, happy, and whole baby; we might have cracked.

The present was all we really had. She was critical, and that's all we could think about or respond to. We learnt to live for the moment and take life as it came. We didn't think about the "What if's...." What if Avelynn had been born normal like Ayla and Kara? What if she didn't have high blood pressure? What if I had done something different during my pregnancy? What if we hadn't had another child? We wouldn't be putting our family through this, and Avelynn wouldn't have existed. But there was no way I'd give her up.

I thought about those questions later; I didn't have the time then. It was a time of extreme stress, and we developed tunnel vision so we could muddle through. What we were going through was hard enough without taking on anything else—a classic response to major stress.

About half past six, I went down to the ICU. I said nothing, just looked at Avelynn with such pain. I thought my heart would burst from the dread, the stress, and anxiety. I expressed milk in a little cubicle in the ICU, listening to great music that cheered me somewhat and helped me to forget where I was. After taking my milk down to the storage room, I properly labelled it, knowing it would otherwise be discarded. Back by Avelynn's side, I caught up on the night's events to learn if she had behaved herself; she had not. Her pressures were still dangerously high, and she was still courageously fighting.

Back in parent accommodation, I joined Peter for breakfast. It was lonely without Ayla and Kara and was the second night without them—the only two I'd ever had. I was relieved that the girls didn't yet have to see their sister and hoped they were enjoying their time with "grandma."

Peter and I went down together to see Avelynn. I will never forget approaching her bed because I couldn't believe what I saw. I looked at her with an overwhelming sense of trepidation and concern, whilst trying to maintain some control over my body. I was not really grasping her new situation. Avelynn looked like she was made of wax. I rapidly began running through scenarios. Was she dead? Why we hadn't been told?

Seeing my look of horror, a nurse quickly interrupted, "Don't be alarmed! We have lowered Avelynn's body temperature to thirty-three degrees Celsius to save her brain." She explained that Avelynn was cooled to reduce the amount oxygen that her brain required, in case of cardiac arrest, which would deprive her of oxygen and potentially damage her brain.

Avelynn was on a cooling pad, inducing mild hypothermia and reducing her rectal temperature to between thirty-three and thirty-five degrees Celsius. As the nurse had explained, it is used on critically ill patients to prevent or mitigate various types of neurologic injury; including brain damage. The cold slows the metabolism, which reduces blood flow and lowers the oxygen requirements of the heart and brain, thus protecting them from damage. The cells require less oxygen at cooler than normal body temperatures.

Once I was reassured, I was sort of okay but really didn't want to see her like that. Who would? Up to this point I hadn't understood that she could have a heart attack. The staff had not run down a list of things that might happen. As I knew that they didn't want anything to happen to her and concentrated making her well.

The reasoning for cooling her helped me to appreciate what they were attempting to do. I appreciated that they were trying to save our baby so we could take her home. Not only take her home but take her home without brain damage. I had never thought of her getting brain damage. This had never occurred to me, that babies could have brain damage after heart surgery.

Only one day after her heart surgery, I was getting a rapid education about what happens behind the closed doors of the ICU. I was learning that I had to stand up, be strong, and deal with all the weird and wonderful things that were happening to Avelynn.

My mind was in a whirl, trying to keep up, and I had no time to prepare for the stress of Avelynn's changing condition. It was all new to me.Nothing had prepared me for this: no books, no movies, and no experiences. In one day, I had learnt more about what happens in the ICU than I ever wanted to know, and wondered what other surprises were in store. I was overwhelmed by how much Avelynn's body could endure. I was privy to things that I did not want to see, but had no choice except to bear it and get through somehow to the other side.

I was relieved a bit that Avelynn seemed more stable with her body temperature lowered. At least her pressures weren't leaping up and down. Leaving Peter to guard her, I visited a physiotherapist at The Royal Women's Hospital, a couple of kilometres up the road, to ask what could be done to help my broken tailbone.

It seemed a minor complaint compared to what Avelynn was fighting, and I felt almost ashamed that I'd even mentioned the pain I was having. It wasn't a time to put myself first, but I could hardly sit without wincing in pain. Because I was expressing, I wouldn't take any drugs for fear it might harm Avelynn. I felt caught between a rock and a hard place.

It had been nine weeks since my coccyx broke during Avelynn's birth, and it so sore. The physio seemed to think it had healed crooked—just my luck. It felt as though I was sitting on a rather large pencil, and I often looked to make sure I wasn't sitting on something. It gave me something to laugh about!

The girls stayed at mum's again—three nights in a row without my beautiful girls to cuddle. Peter and I decided to have take-away because it was too easy not to. I'm already over it, our usual dinner is meat, our vegetables or salad, and rice and pasta. Pretty simple food really, without the greasy oil that can be hard to avoid in take-away food.

Peter and I were only slightly more optimistic, but we were working on automatic. We hardly spoke to each other and spoke only briefly with our friends in Perth who phoned. We were reserved, not wanting to give false hope that Avelynn would survive. Peter's parents 'phoned that night. I let him talk to them, explaining that things were okay for the moment but could change at any time. It really wasn't fun talking to anyone.

Peter and I went to bed after visiting our beautiful little girl with her wonderful auburn hair and telling to behave. On the way out of the ICU, towards the lifts to the parents' accommodation, there was a cafe/shop that was open late. Every night I'd buy myself a jam donut. I developed a superstition that if the shop had no jam donuts, then things would be bad for Avelynn. Somehow, there was a jam donut waiting for me every night. I thought that was a fantastic omen.

My second day in ICU. I still require lots of drug support.

Avelynn's diary, Wednesday, 17 November 1999

Chapter 18

Pulmonary Hypertension and onto ECMO

Avelynn had a cardiac arrest—seven minutes—at 11.05 A.M. She's very unstable due to putting saline down tube to lung and sucking it out again. The nurses had to do a swab to grow cultures.

Nurses now scared to do suction.

From Peter: "A day of bad news. Both Michelle and myself are in an state of emotional shock. Both of us are quite teary for short periods of time, but we are strong. The concrete floor feels like it is made of rubber and sinks as you walk—a time of extreme stress"

My diary, Thursday, 18 November 1999

As was my habit, I woke at half past six and went directly to the ICU before coffee or breakfast. I always popped my head in to see my precious baby, to give her a quick kiss and to let her know I'm there for her. I then checked with the duty nurse on the night's activities and expressed my breast milk. When I saw Avelynn, I noticed she'd been taken off the cold pad and she looked more like herself, not like wax dummy she represented yesterday. So I felt relieved and welcomed what I took to be a positive event.

Since Avelynn had come into the ICU on Tuesday, she was on drugs that paralysed her muscles (so she couldn't move) as well as drugs (such as morphine and pain killers) to heavily sedate her. She also received a cocktail of other drugs, which kept her alive. Though it's probably naive, I liked to think of her in a wonderful, magic-fairy dreamland where she was comfortable and secure., sustained by memories of us—of our short but sweet life with her—loving and supporting her. Giving her the strength to carry on and not feel so alone in the drug haze. I wondered where she went to escape what was happening and if she was conscious of any pain.

Peter and I came back down to the ICU after breakfast—without Ayla and Kara once again. I gave her another kiss on the forehead and held her hand. To my surprise, it was as if she were determined to wake up and greet us. She started to blink her eyes and move her lips like she was trying to form an "O" shape with them.

It was the first time I'd seen her do that, and I thought it was cute. My attitude didn't last long after I told her nurse, "Hey, Avelynn's blinking her eyes and moving her lips. Wow, she's moving!" The nurse leapt to attention and hurriedly gave her another dose of the muscle paralysing drug, saying, "She's not allowed to do that."

I was really scared and worried. I hadn't realised that Avelynn shouldn't move, that any movement was potentially life-threatening. Because her pressures were incredibly unstable, they had the potential to go up or down at any moment like a kid's seesaw. This was the main reason she was on the muscle relaxant in the first place; she was too critical to twitch a muscle and so unstable that the slightest movement could trigger a heart attack.

It dawned on me then just how critical and fragile was Avelynn's hold on life. The nurse cautioned us not to touch Avelynn any more, not even on her hand or foot. It's bloody hard for a parent to think that touching your child could kill them. All we wanted to do was nurture and protect her, but we couldn't even touch her. Even the cleaning lady had to be careful not to bump her cot in case she set Avelynn into cardiac arrest.

I was terrified and felt guilty that I had been touching and talking to her. Somehow it was my fault that she was so unstable, and I had contributed to her predicament. I felt so protective of her and thought I was reassuring her, but I didn't consider the consequences. I suppose the nurse didn't realise either what effect my voice or my light touch would have on her. Thinking that Avelynn could have a heart attack and not be with us any longer, was hard to comprehend, but it scared the life out of me.

That didn't stop me from wanting to pick her up, to trade places with her, and give her all my love and strength. I had thought I could manage, or that I would be stronger. But no matter how much we wanted to, no amount of wishful thinking could change the fact that she was fighting for her life every second. It was almost unbearable. Yesterday, we'd had a reprieve, but now her pressures were still unstable. Today threatened to become a nightmare.

I was almost relieved when Peter and I were invited to the regular Thursday morning ICU tea. I thought that if I were not with Avelynn she could just rest and behave herself. She wouldn't be trying to move or to communicate with me. At the time, I was a bit panicky and not thinking quite right, but it made sense to me.

The Thursday morning tea was a time to speak with other parents in the ICU, and the chaplain was there in case you wanted to speak to her. If you really needed her, the chaplain was usually available. It was great talking to a couple of people about what was going on in the ICU. We could not speak yet about Avelynn; it was still too painful. We spoke in generalities: about living in the ICU, what the coffee was like, and how marvellous the nurses were.

We hadn't yet had any opportunitys to talk to other parents; we'd spent every waking moment with Avelynn or eating. or for me, expressing and storing my breast milk. In the ICU, we focused on Avelynn and didn't socialise with other parents, even to say, "Hi there, how are you?" It wasn't a case of being rude; I couldn't deal with anyone else's sick child when I could hardly deal with mine. I could not handle the emotions surrounding what I was going through.

I couldn't have coped if they'd told me they were feeling poorly. It's not that I had ignored them; I'd give a quick smile of encouragement when we passed in the corridor or while sitting at our child's bedside. But I wasn't capable of having a conversation that required any thought. Thinking took energy that I didn't have. That was how my brain worked: I didn't want to know what was going on around me or to know what was wrong with anyone else's child.

At the morning tea, I avoided those types of questions and side -stepped those that I didn't want to answer. You may think that a bit odd, but I was too frightened to talk about Avelynn and couldn't communicate normally with anyone. I enjoyed a brief respite from the normal day-to-day ICU activity and sharing a coffee amongst people going through a similar time. Peter and I had barely finished our coffee when one of the nurses grabbed us, told us we were to come quickly, and dragged us down the corridor. A couple of doctor were waiting to talk to us.

As we entered the room, we looked at the doctors' faces: it wasn't good news. Their eyes were filled with compassion, and I knew they didn't want to tell us, but they had to. They explained that Avelynn had a heart attack whilst we were having morning tea. Oh my God. It was such a hard concept to grasp that our baby had a major heart attack at nine weeks. The doctors were trying to tell us, as gently as possible, that they had struggled to revive her. Her open chest helped immensely; they were able to do cardiac massage directly on her heart. Somehow, she defied the odds. She courageously fought her way back from the brink after seven long minutes with no heart beat.

Pressure was growing in my chest, and a lump was growing in my throat. I found it hard to breathe, and I pinched my lips together, pressed my tongue hard up against the top of my mouth, and tried to stifle my unwanted tears. I had to face the doctors and what they were saying, but it was a hard reality.

I was sad and angry at the same time, but I didn't want to burst into tears. Part of me wanted to break down or start screaming obscenities. Trying to maintain some control, I thought, "How the hell did this happen?" "Surely, this couldn't be happening to Avelynn!" It was so awful, so incredibly hard to grasp.

The doctors explained that they were fairly confident that she had received enough oxygen to prevent brain damage, but they couldn't rule it out. It was miraculous, they told us; the blood samples (called "blood gases") that they took during those seven long minutes when her heart wasn't beating showed her oxygen levels were okay.

The brain is quite susceptible to oxygen deprivation, and each minute that your brain is without oxygen reduces your chance of living. Even a brief lack of oxygen can cause irreversible brain damage. I was, at least, relieved knowing she was in the best place, with doctors and nurses properly trained to do cardiac massage immediately available. We could only hope her brain was protected when she was resuscitated.

Seven minutes is a long time for her heart not to beat. I was worried and scared about the consequences. Before that, I hadn't realised that a heart attack could cause brain damage. I innocently thought that if you did Cardiopulmonary Resuscitation (CPR) that the brain would get enough oxygen

I hadn't realised that wasn't the case, that CPR had to be done properly so the brain could get enough oxygen. Ironically, I had thought it was the heart that needed saving, but apparently brain cells die more quickly than heart muscles. Brain cells die within minutes; some articles say within three minutes, others say within six-to-nine minutes. Newborns and young children seem to be more resilient. It was time for a reality check for Michelle; not that I needed another one.

My world had been shattered again. Attempting to grasp this information felt like a physical blow. My legs buckled, and I swayed back and forth, trying to concentrate on controlling myself. Surely this couldn't be actually happening to us! Why had we been thrust into this position, and what about our future with Avelynn? Was there going to be one? What about the dream I had of her making it through this ordeal? Thinking was hard, and I became numb. My tears were frozen. It was as if I were on automatic pilot.

This was the pivotal point for Peter and me as we came to understand what the doctors meant. They explained what her unstable pressures meant and the very real chance of not bringing Avelynn home. It was as if Avelynn were wrestling with an unknown demonic creature that controlled her pulmonary and arterial pressures and wouldn't let go.

This fight wasn't for the faint hearted; it was real, it was hard, and we couldn't afford to lose. It became the focus of our entire universe. We never gave up hope. Somehow, we must manage to show the same courage as Avelynn. Not scream, not pass out, but just hack it, and focus on our love and gratitude for Avelynn, for the ICU staff, and for each other. Otherwise, we had nothing to hold on to.

Although the surgeons had successfully repaired Avelynn's congenital heart defect, truncus arteriosus, she was not yet out of the woods. In some cases of truncus, pulmonary vascular resistance disease has already begun, which causes right ventricular failure—heart failure—and premature death from a heart attack. In children born with normal circulation, the pulmonary artery comes from the right ventricle and the aorta comes from the left ventricle. The arteries are completely separate. Coronary arteries, which supply blood to the heart muscle, originate at the aorta, just above the heart.

Truncus arteriosus occurs when the pulmonary artery and the aorta don't form properly. Instead they formed one large vessel. This vessel, called the truncus, carries blood both to the body and the lungs. The truncus forms over a large opening called a ventricular septal defect (VSD). The VSD is a hole in the wall between the heart's two pumping chambers: the lower ventricles. As a result, the blue blood (without oxygen) and the red blood- (oxygen rich) blood mix.

Before corrective surgery, some of this mixed blood goes to the lungs, some goes to the rest of the body, and some goes to the coronary arteries. Too much blood is sent to the lungs. Over time, the extra blood flow damages the blood vessels to the lungs and the vessels in the lungs. This damage is permanent and over time makes it difficult for the heart to pump blood to the lungs. It's a bit like a garden hose that's partially blocked; you have to open the tap to increase the water flow. When this happens to the lungs, the required pressure gets higher and higher, making the right side of the heart work harder and harder.

Closing the VSD—the large hole in her heart—caused massive pressure to build up in her pulmonary arterial (PA) system, the blood that flows to her lungs. PA pressure should only be around fifteen millimetres of mercury or so, and the heart pressure is always greater than that in normal circumstances. But because the high pressure caused by truncus, Avelynn developed pulmonary vascular resistance disease, also called pulmonary hypertension.

After surgery to repair truncus, the lungs typically calm down and the PA pressures drop to near normal within a few days. Unfortunately, Avelynn's PA pressures showed no signs of dropping, even with massive drug support. Her pressures could quickly rise again, as they had that morning. If her PA pressures rose, she would have another heart attack unless the staff acted quickly to prevent it. Unfortunately, as the doctors explained, there is no cure for pulmonary hypertension. They could only hope that her lungs stopped being so reactive, and that her pressures came down over time. That's if they could keep her alive long enough.

Avelynn needed a miracle; she had one heart attack and was at risk of another at any time. She also had a lot of bleeding from her chest and had collapsed lobes on both lungs. Her lungs had collapsed as a result of the CPR she had. But, she still had a fighting chance. There are occasional news stories of children surviving in extraordinary circumstances—stories of miracles. It was our turn. Avelynn needed a miracle, and we could only dream about it happening.

We were well beyond wishful thinking and were desperately thinking. We were fraught with fear, yet I never gave up hope of her getting better, of her somehow pulling out of this predicament and overcoming the overwhelming odds. I refused to believe otherwise. Religious people believe in a divinity that regulates this world. They believe there is something beyond us—but I don't know. We were praying, with all our might, to a power greater than us; praying that Avelynn would survive.

Peter and I kept keeping each other's spirits up although we felt numb. Time ceased to have any meaning. The future and the past became irrelevant as we lived solely for the moment. It became our living nightmare, a nightmare that didn't vanish when we woke. Our grief was unrelenting and worry over the fate of our brave little girl tried to suffocate us. In my heart, I never gave up believing Avelynn would come home with her two older sisters, because I couldn't imagine how they would live without their baby sister.

With that in mind, I placed a beautiful picture of Avelynn with Ayla and Kara, taken just before we'd left Perth, and hung it on her ICU bed. Back in the ICU room, I asked a nurse for some sticky tape to attach the gorgeous picture to her bed. "What you do want that for," she asked. "Well this is a picture I took only a week ago. You see Avelynn? Well that's the baby we want to come home with us to Perth. We want her back like that, whole and well, with nothing wrong." The nurse looked weirdly at me, slightly unbelieving, as though to say, "Yep, sure! We'll do our best but there are no guarantees." I didn't care what anyone thought, I was her mum.

Peter and I took shifts reading to Avelynn throughout the day. It comforted us to think that if she could hear us, she would know we hadn't deserted her. I somehow thought if we stayed by her side and talked to her, she would decide to stay in this world and not go to the next. That bloody song, "Knock, Knock, Knockin on Heaven's Door" kept going around and around in my head, like the record had broken. I wanted it out of my head but it wouldn't go away; it was only that snippet. When I mentioned this to the ICU nurse, she looked at me as though I had lost it.

I hope the nurses didn't think we were checking up on them by sitting with Avelynn all day. We tried to keep out of their way, but occasionally it was difficult. When Avelynn's PA pressure rose, nurses and doctors all seemed to rush around Avelynn's bed. I tried to get out of the way, standing away from her bed so they could reach her. Sadly these episodes were all too frequent: Avelynn's pressures rose too high, she had another heart attack, nearly had another heart attack, her heart went into arrhythmia (irregular heart rhythm), or was about to go into arrhythmia.

Tracheal suctioning is an essential part of airway management for intubated critically ill patients. Suctioning removes thick mucus and secretions from the trachea and lower airway that otherwise can't be moved. It helped her breathe better by controlling the build-up of mucus in her lungs, that were still partly collapsed from her recent CPR. However, the nurses were reluctant to do the suctioning, which had triggered her cardiac arrest that morning. Nevertheless, the suctioning was essential. Without it, oxygen couldn't properly reach her lungs. Catch-22.

As usual, I spent most of my time glancing up and down from the book I was reading, keeping a constant eye on the monitor screen which showed her PA pressures. The same monitor also showed her systemic pressure (blood pressure), heart rate, oxygen saturation, and her respiratory rate (how frequently she breathed). At that time, her breathing rate was controlled by the ventilator.

As I stared unbelieving, her PA pressure suddenly began to quickly rise. It had been about 50 but suddenly jumped to 60, 75, 91, 101, 115. Bang! She was having another heart attack right in front of me. I leapt up out of my chair, saying to the nurse, "Bugger! Shit! Shall I go?" Not the best language, but the nurse said, "If you can hack it, stay!"

My right leg was forward, my left leg was back, and I felt like going and staying at the same time. I felt useless. My thoughts were racing, "What if I go, and she doesn't make it?" "Can I hack seeing her die?" "Where the bloody hell is Peter when I need him?" "Can I keep watching the ICU team fight for her life and keep giving her drugs? What if I pass out?" "Gees, I need chocolate." "I wish I knew what to do." In reality I hadn't moved more than a metre-and-a-half from her bed, and I hadn't spoken again. "It's okay, mum!" The ICU staff often called us all mum, as they couldn't be expected to remember all our names, and it seemed appropriate. "You can sit back down again, but that was a close call." Peter rushed in, shocked to learn what had happened. Like me, he squared his shoulders and thought, we have to hang in there and be as brave as Avelynn. Peter took over from me and started reading to her.

It was my turn with Ayla and Kara. They were seemed to be okay, although Kara kept asking, "Why doesn't my baby wake up?" "Why does she have things in her mouth?" They were content with my answers and didn't know how critical their baby was. I don't think it would have helped, and none of us knew the final outcome.

I did not see the point of telling the girls, who were so young, that their baby, Avelynn might not be coming home. Children at that age see everything in black and white, there's no grey, and Avelynn's condition was definitely in the grey. The ICU isn't a place for young, healthy siblings to spend much time. After they'd seen Avelynn, I took the girls to a park about 200 metres from the hospital. The park is just past the car park and the Ronald McDonald houses where other families stay with long time hospital residents.

The park had the basics, and I had fun chasing the girls around the play equipment. It was great being out in the fresh air. I had my mobile phone and knew the ICU staff would ring me if anything happened to Avelynn. It was great to be outdoors, chasing the girl, trying not to worry about my baby in the ICU, trying to be a normal parent, and having fun with my two older kids.

About an hour later, I arrived back in the ICU, and Peter told me Avelynn had another close call but the staff had asked him to leave the room. When I queried the nurse, she said that Peter went as white as a ghost, and they had been afraid that he might pass out. It's ironic really that Peter, the SASR man trained to fight battles, trained to make split second decisions in the midst of full-on adrenaline experiences, wasn't prepared to hack his baby having a heart attack. I am not trained for combat, but I could manage this. Perhaps my background had given me more strength and courage than I knew; the staff often commented on how strong I was.

That was something to consider another time. For now, I seemed to carry on despite all Avelynn was going through. In reality, Peter and I relied on each other's strength for support. Without Peter's support, I wouldn't have got on as well. Peter and I got strength from Avelynn as well. We said, if she can hack it then so can we—ours was the easy job.

Around eleven-thirty, the staff told me to get out and said that someone would ring if anything untoward happened. I wasn't really doing anything anyway, and needed my sleep so I could continue to cope and be there if I was needed. What an intense day! I hoped the next day would be better. As usual, I went to the shop on the second floor and was relieved to find my jam donut. I took it as a good omen. Maybe I was clutching at straws.

> **Oh, dear! I am in trouble after tracheal suction. I had a pulmonary hypertension crisis. My blood pressure is the same as my pulmonary artery pressure, and I am bleeding. I gave mum and dad a fright.**
>
> **Avelynn's diary, Thursday, 18 November 1999**

> **Avelynn had another episode—a heart attack—lasting approximately four minutes this morning. Heart didn't stop this time, but needed adrenaline. I saw it again; freaky stuff. The ICU staff decided to put adrenaline down her tracheal**

tube before they suctioned in an attempt to stop her having heart attacks. She's got a collapsed right lung; top lobe. She's really still critical and the staff can't do any physio to relieve the lung. The lung has fluid build up in it and the nurses hate to suction it out in case she goes into cardiac arrest.

They need to turn her but she won't tolerate even her head being moved. The doctors, Peter, and I had big discussions about putting Avelynn on ECMO—a heart-lung machine—to keep her stable. Aggressive medication with an adrenaline drip didn't work so they took her off that. My brother, Rowen, arrived with his wife and two kids. My sister is here with her youngest child, a baby only three months older than Avelynn. At six this evening, I showed Avelynn to Rowen. Her pressures were still unstable.

The staff told me to get Peter immediately. We discussed putting Avelynn on ECMO as basically she's going to die if we don't. She has one-to-three days to live if she makes it past tonight. Wow! We weren't told about this one in Perth. We're really upset—nerves at the tip of my fingers are tingling, I'm shaking, I feel like my heart has been ripped out. The risks of going on ECMO are cardiac arrest and brain damage. There's nothing else to do except give her a chance to live and put her on ECMO. I still have hope and if there is a God I hope he's looking after her. She's a fighter, and I still believe in my heart we will take her back home with us.

We were told to have her christened, as the odds were stacked against her. If she didn't die tonight going on ECMO, that was probably a miracle in itself. There was maybe a fifty percent chance she would die and a higher chance she would have a heart attack or brain damage. It was risky business, and the only reason we agreed was because if we didn't then we had already signed her death warrant. We had no choice so we chose a slim chance at life over no life. We also didn't get her christened because Ayla and Kara hadn't been, and we thought it would be hypocritical of us if we did. We thought if there is a God then he'll know, and she doesn't need to be christened to prove anything.

> **Avelynn went on ECMO at half-past eight, and it took until half-past ten to have her fully on. It's working well with no complications so far. It's hard to see her like that and is overwhelming for us that I can hardly stand it. This was probably the closest I've come to cracking up.**
>
> **We went to bed after spending some time sitting with her and telling her that she can fight the pulmonary hypertension and enjoy living with us once again. Peter and I were so stressed, we couldn't talk, not even to each other.**
>
> **My diary, Friday, 19 November 1999**

I woke early and went straight downstairs to see my beautiful little girl. On the way to the ICU, I thought that because we hadn't received a phone call last night, Avelynn might have finally turned the corner. I quickly said "hello" to her then expressed, and took my milk to the storage room. Looking at all the stored bottles, I wondered if Avelynn would ever drink any. I expressed 600-to-800 millilitres a day and absently wondered if the hospital could use my milk for another child if Avelynn couldn't use it. That was only a flicker of a thought; I couldn't dwell on the negatives. I was living in constant fear of Avelynn being taken from us.

Back in the ICU, I looked at Avelynn, keeping an eye on her PA pressure, wishing they'd stay down, and trying not to touch her in case I set her pressures off again. I was clutching at straws—Avelynn had another episode lasting for around four minutes. Her heart didn't stop this time, but a cardiac arrest is still a cardiac arrest. I had to wonder how much more she could take. Even one of the nurses said, "There are only so many times a person can be bought back." Numb with fear, I watched my tough little cookie pull through yet again.

Avelynn had quite a few cardiac arrests as a result of her pulmonary hypertension. That should have gone away after her heart surgery, but didn't. One of her doctors pulled a double shift, searching the Internet for anything that could possibly help. This morning, on my way to see Avelynn, I saw the same doctor whom I had seen at half-past eleven the night before. He was in the same position and on the same computer. I asked him, "Are you still on the computer from last night?" "Yes," he said, "and I have not slept."

It seemed unreal; this guy was my champion. He spent all night on that computer, looking for something to get our baby out of her trouble. I couldn't believe what he had put himself through, and how the other ICU staff were digging within themselves to come up with answers to save our baby. These doctors are truly amazing; they are incredible human beings and our unsung heroes. They are among the most altruistic people I've ever met, giving their time, not even sleeping, because Avelynn needed an answer. They were searching the world.

Avelynn seemed to have that effect on people. No matter who they are, people want to help her. Maybe because she is special, she reminds us all that we can fight if we have the guts to stick to it, be strong, and trust in those around us. That the universe is working with us and not against us. We must believe in love, gratitude, and miracles. Peter and I are so grateful to those wonderful, caring souls who looked after Avelynn and didn't give up hope for her future. Without them, she wouldn't be here.

To lower her PA pressures, and to prevent more cardiac arrests (although her heart was incredibly strong to have so survived so far) the doctors decided to drip a half millilitre of adrenalin down her trachea tube (the tube in her throat) every hour or so. I thought I had seen everything, but the bloody pressures wouldn't come down. The adrenalin made no difference. Her pressures were extremely persistent.

Today the staff explained to us a machine called extracorporeal membrane oxygenation (ECMO). We were told if Avelynn wasn't put on an ECMO, she wouldn't live to see the weekend out. They doubted her heart could handle much more abuse, and I agreed with them. It was a miracle she had made it this far. Her strong but battered heart had earned a rest.

The ICU staff thought she wouldn't make it and wanted us to have her christened. They called the chaplain down to speak with us. Although she was lovely, and we respected her, we choose not to have Avelynn christened. It seemed hypocritical of us, since Ayla and Kara weren't. Peter and I were christened as children; it just seemed like it was something our parents did because it was what was expected back in our day.

Nowadays, many parents don't have their children christened because they want their children to make up their own minds. I've nothing against christening; I just didn't think it was the right time or place, and would have been hypocritical. I have always lived by my ethos, and thought this was against it. But having declined the kind offer, we still received a lot of comfort from the Chaplain that night.

We spoke with her about the fight Avelynn was having, and the possibility of losing her. We discussed our two older children; that it was important to include them in Avelynn's hospital stay as much as we could without upsetting them. One way we did that was to buy Tigger for Kara to give Avelynn as a hospital present. Ayla gave her a Christmas teddy bear that I bought from the great shop downstairs. If Avelynn died, the girls could choose either to let Avelynn keep their stuffed toys to take with her to heaven or keep themselves as a reminder of their baby. The Chaplain seemed to think that was a smart idea and thought it would be a great comfort to the girls.

At six, when I showed Avelynn to my brother, Rowan, her pressures were really unstable. He'd just arrived at the hospital with his wife and two children, aged four and nine years. My older sister had also arrived with her four-year-old daughter and little baby boy, only three months older than Avelynn.

Rowan was the only one in the ICU with me. Peter was with my sister. The doctor asked me to get Peter and asked Rowan to leave. It was apparent that Avelynn had no choice except to be put onto ECMO. Her little heart had fought valiantly, but we all knew it couldn't take much more of a beating. I think she'd had four or five heart attacks in four days. The ICU nurse had told me that there were only so many times they could bring her back.

It didn't help that we did not fully comprehend what ECMO entailed. We were not able to visualise it. We were told this was the absolute last ditch chance of saving Avelynn. What choice did we have? We knew that ECMO was a type of heart-lung machine that would give Avelynn's heart and lungs a rest. More important, we knew we had no other options available. If we wanted a chance of saving our daughter, this was it. There was no Plan C.

There was no reprisal either way we chose. I know the doctors had given us the facts; they were brutally honest with us as we had asked them to be. But it was our choice, and they were relying on Peter and me to make this important decision with the knowledge that we'd just gotten from them. Our stress and anxiety were extremely high. I knew if we made the wrong decision, I'd punish myself forever. I take responsibilities extremely seriously, and I knew Peter usually relied on me to make decisions. Therefore, I felt the decision was on my head.

The doctors had explained that putting Avelynn onto ECMO would give her heart and lungs a chance to rest for a couple of days and allow her lung pressure to return to near normal. ECMO was a last resort; it carried serious risks even when performed by skilled and experienced hospital staff. There is a high risk of infection and haemorrhaging; her blood had to be thinned out by anticoagulant drugs, such as heparin. Because Avelynn's risk of death was greater than the risk of ECMO, we had no choice.

"Okay, who's going to sign the papers to put her onto ECMO," one of the doctors asked. The papers had to be signed for legal purposes as the hospital didn't want us coming back at them for anything. However, we knew the pain the doctors were in recommending the right treatment for Avelynn. This was the only course of action they could think of to save her. "Who's going to sign," they asked again; time was ticking by. "Michelle, I will," Peter said, "you signed for her surgery." After Peter signed, he gave Avelynn a quick kiss and walked straight out. He could no longer stand the stress.

The look on the nurses' faces said it all: our baby had to fight a massive battle, unlike any she'd already gone through and probably would not come out of the procedure alive. I was numb; I couldn't believe it had come to this. I was shivering with fright and such apprehension as I'd never known before. I held Avelynn's little hand in mine, trying to inject my strength into her, trying to let her know that I was there for her.

Five minutes previously, one of the nurses had said to me, "Michelle, we've woken her up a little bit, so you can say good-bye. She might not be able to see you, but she can hear you." The ICU staff was giving me a chance to say good-bye; they honestly didn't believe she would come through the procedure. This was a precious gift, and I knew she could hear me. She was trying to focus her eyes on me through the drug haze. As I stared into her face, I was trying to picture her vibrant, alive, and whole. I knew she'd responded to me, and we'd had a very special moment—mum and baby together.

I was terrified of her fragile condition and didn't want to waste any time, fearing she would have another cardiac arrest or bleed, so I didn't prolong our time together. I made sure Avelynn had "Tigger" with her, told her she'd be alright, and promised I would see her after she was on ECMO. One of the nurses said, "It's okay. You can spend some more time with her." By the look on her face, she was thinking that it would be the last time I would spend with Avelynn.

It's not that the nurse deliberately did or said anything to give away her feelings; it's just that I am very perceptive, reading body language and voice tone. My senses were razor sharp when it came to Avelynn's survival, even though my brain seemingly had switched off all other faculties. But I was confident—mostly.

I remembered the dream in which Avelynn faced death but miraculously survived. Although I still had my heart in my mouth and nerves were tingling at the tips of my fingers, I had nothing to hold onto except my intuition. She just had to pull through, give her all, and fight with every cell in her body. Like Peter had just done, I quickly kissed her cheek and hand, and made a hasty getaway before I changed my mind.

I walked out of the room, feeling as though my heart had been ripped out. It suddenly felt as though an enormous weight had been placed on my chest. I could hardly breathe, I couldn't speak, I couldn't see for my tears, but I couldn't cry. I was nearly paralysed with fear and ready to break down, but I didn't want Avelynn to sense my fear; she needed to be strong. Although I knew she might not see me again, I had to leave the ICU. I had to get out of there.

ECMO is an advanced life-support system which took over the role of Avelynn's heart and lungs, providing them with desperately needed rest. It also took over the role of her kidneys, filtering her blood. Avelynn's ECMO was manufactured by Legacy Health Systems, who describe its function.

> Putting a child on ECMO is a sophisticated procedure similar to the heart-lung bypass machine used in cardiac surgery. ECMO takes over the oxygenation and heart function in children who have advanced lung or cardiac disease or have suffered severe trauma. Unlike a mechanical ventilator, which forces oxygen into the lungs, the ECMO machine diverts blood out of the body and through an oxygenator that removes carbon dioxide and adds oxygen to the blood. The blood is returned to the body through cannulas where it provides oxygen to the patient's heart, brain, and other vital organs.

ECMO is an invasive treatment, generally used as a procedure of last resort for patients who would not survive without it. It may be used for a periods of several hours to several days; in extreme cases may be used for several weeks. As the lungs and heart recover, the patient is first weaned from the ECMO, then the machine is removed. This is what the doctors were planning for Avelynn.

At half-past eight, the ICU staff started the procedure of putting Avelynn on ECMO. She was too critical to move into the theatre, so the staff asked all of the visitors to leave and did the whole procedure in the ICU.

Rowan kept vigil with Peter and me that night, while mum and Sharon looked after Ayla and Kara, feeding them a late dinner. We waited in a little room furnished with two chairs and a two-seater that could be unfolded to provide a bed for parents who had nowhere else to sleep. The room was on the left, just outside the ICU and just across the hall from a handy toilet. We drank tea and coffee, and I zoned out. Rowan and Peter chatted about work; Peter was in the army, as Rowan had been for fifteen years or so. We sat there, waiting to be told whether she had died or miraculously survived.

I must have gone to the toilet a thousand times; it gave me something to do. My hands had taken on a life of their own—they wouldn't do what I wanted. They felt supercharged with electricity, as if they had a thousand bolts running through them. The pain was excruciating and lasted for hours.

Someone told me that I was trying to give Avelynn my energy such as in *Reiki*. Whatever it was, it hurt. Rowan, Peter, and I (especially) spoke very little; talking wasn't any use, and I was conserving my energy. We were suspended in time between fear, hope, and the future. A ringing phone broke the silence, and my heart leapt with fright. I would have let it ring; I couldn't answer, so Peter did. The doctor told him, "She's stable for now; we've managed to transfer her onto ECMO. You can see her if you would like." "Oh, my God! Let's hope she's okay, because I can't take much more !" I said, and Peter agreed. We all gave each other a cuddle, too numb to cry, but relief showed on our faces.

We thanked Rowan for staying with us, and are eternally grateful for his support that night, and for mum looking after the kids. Rowan left, with our thanks, headed to the parents' accommodation to try to sleep. Peter and I went to see Avelynn and to make sure she was actually doing okay.

As I mentioned, we didn't really know what ECMO was, and we hadn't seen a picture of a child on the machine. It's true: a picture is worth a thousand words. If I'd seen a picture, I might have been better prepared to see Avelynn for the first time on ECMO. But I wasn't prepared at all—not mentally or physically prepared for the shock. Entering her room, I didn't comprehend at first what I saw. My Avelynn appeared to be sleeping amongst massive machines, and I felt my knees buckle.

I was tried to gain control of my body. My eyes wide, I tried and take it all in. Tears sprang from my eyes, rolling unchecked down my face and obscuring my view. My throat closed, making it impossible to talk, and there was a loud roar in my ears. I slowly approached her side, making sure I wasn't in the vicinity of any tubes in case I fainted. I was light-headed and, I am ashamed to admit, a little grossed-out.

The sight was hard to comprehend. I was mesmerised by the sight of blood in the cannulas attached to her neck. In one, blood was the usual colour, but in the other, the colour was very dark. I had been told she'd be attached to the machine, but the sight of her blood in the tubes freaked me out. My right hand was over my mouth while my left wiped unwanted tears from my eyes.

I had thought machines like this were science-fiction, not real, and certainly not attached to my precious baby. I didn't think I would pass out, but I felt sorely tested. The sight of her attached to this machine, now acting as her external heart, lungs and kidneys, scared me deeply. I felt trapped in a horror movie. I couldn't handle seeing her like that and closed down in some kind of shock. After a couple of minutes, I ran from her room. Not long after, Peter followed.

Looking at Avelynn and this ECMO that was keeping her alive, was a real shock—the stuff of nightmares. I had to make a mental adjustment, and I had better get used to it damn quickly so I that could support my baby. I felt ultimately responsible for the well-being of my children, especially Avelynn, and was filled with guilt and self accusation. I was angry, but with no one at fault for Avelynn's predicament, I got really pissed-off at myself.

It was hard to see Avelynn like that. Still overwhelmed, I went back in with Peter and sat down next to her, still too scared to touch her. I told her that she can fight the pulmonary hypertension and enjoy living with us once again. Peter and I eventually left her side with a promise from the nurses to call us if anything happened.

As usual, I told Peter to go on ahead. I needed to express and to buy my lucky chocolate jam donut.

> **I had a head scan. My chest is not so good and I am misbehaving badly. Now, they have to do another ECHO—ultra sound on the heart—and worse still, the doctors think I have to go on ECMO- Extra Corporeal Membrane Oxygenator. ECMO is a form of support for my lungs and heart.**
>
> **Finally I have to go onto ECMO with lots of support.**
>
> **Avelynn's diary, Friday, 19 November 1999**

> **Sharon slept over with Rory, and Peter shared Ayla's pull out bed though it was a tight squeeze. Ayla and Kara are happy to have a baby to play with in bed and Rory smiled and played with them happy with the attention he was getting. It was sad for me to watch them play with a healthy baby when Avelynn was fighting so hard in the ICU, and her future so uncertain. The girls love Avelynn very much and love playing babies, so I was grateful they had their small cousin to play with and to cheer them.**
>
> **I got up at five, unable to stay in bed any longer, and went downstairs to see Avelynn. As soon as I saw her, the tears rolled down my face and I let them. It's hard to take watching her like that, my poor baby. Felt bad today, as if my chest would burst.**

Mum arrived with Kim and Marcus. They all saw Avelynn. They didn't come close, and I could tell it was hard for them to see her like that.

Peter and I can barely function at this point and asked mum to look after the girls for us for two nights. I didn't like the idea of them being away, but it was for the best. Mum didn't mind and hopefully they would enjoy their stay at grandma's better than hanging around the ICU with sad parents who weren't much fun to be with.

Peter and I took it in turns, singing nursery rhymes to Avelynn and generally talking to her about her sisters, our home in Perth, and things in general. Her pressures are lower on ECMO so I feel a little relieved.

My diary, Saturday, 20 November 1999

My sister Sharon had asked last night if it was okay to bring Rory and stay overnight to offer some support and help out with the girls. I know she was really thinking, "What if the situation was turned around, and it was her in hospital praying Rory would get better?" I was envious that she had a healthy bouncing baby boy while Avelynn had seemed to cop the works. But that's life;

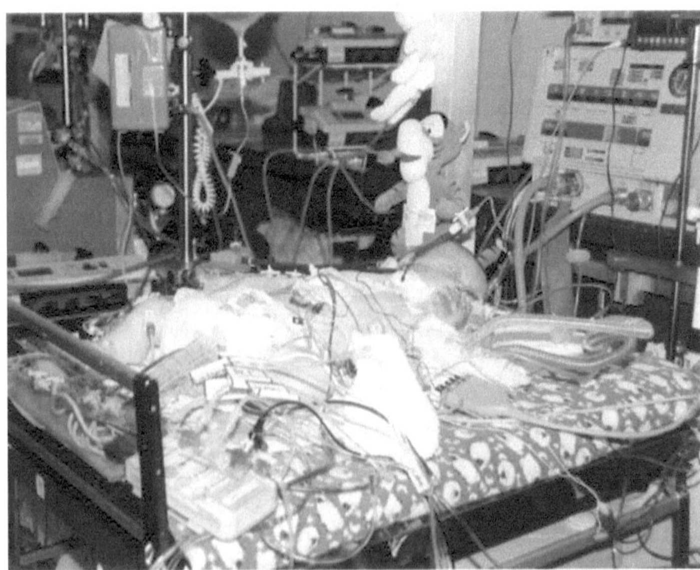

Avelynn on ECMO

there's no use complaining. I was really pleased Ayla and Kara had a baby to play with whom to play.

I got up really early and went down to the ICU to see Avelynn. It is still hard for me to see her like that. It's overwhelming. This is such an abnormal way to see a child. I know Avelynn is not out of the woods yet; she has only a slim chance of surviving, even with the help of ECMO.

It seemed to me that when Avelynn was on ECMO, every second that she gained heading in the right direction was another second that we had her. I couldn't manage my feelings. My brain said, "Well, I'll just shut your feelings down while cope." That's pretty much what happened: Peter and I went numb from stress.

By that point, we had been through so much. From when I first got pregnant, learning about having a child with congenital heart disease, handing our baby over to the surgeons only a couple of days previously (it felt like years), to this moment. Waiting for her pressures to somehow go down and miraculously stay down. Peter and I held it together as best we could. I felt dizzy today, as though I would, wondering whether I would ever wake up it I did faint.

Today was a blur. Mum came with Kim and Marcus, and they wanted to see Avelynn. It was a shock for them see her like that, even though they did not get close. They only glimpsed her from the doorway. Mum took the girls; we weren't much use and certainly no fun to be around. We hoped they would have a better time at grandma's.

Today Avelynn seemed to be doing better and her pressures were lower—closer to normal. It was still hard to see her like that, but a doctor gave us a fantastic book to read out loud to Avelynn. *Politically Incorrect Fairy Tales* was hilarious. With themes running through the book such as little red riding hood being eaten by the wolf—a quick and clever carnivore.

I spent the day waiting for anything to happen. We were so used to lots of events occurring around Avelynn that we had grown unaccustomed to nothing happening. I was expecting Avelynn to do something and for the nurses and doctors to respond. I wasn't used to the nurses calmly going about their business with Avelynn. The perfusionist seemed extremely confident, monitoring the ECMO, ensuring all was well. Reading aloud from a wacky book was just the thing. It tickled my fancy because I have a very wacky sense of humour, and it was great to be reading aloud to Avelynn. Letting her hear my voice felt like I was reaching out to her, and she wasn't on her own.

Comedy and tragedy come together; no matter how hard I laughed, our precious baby was still attached to this machine, still fighting for her life, and still looking awful. The long tubes in her neck were covered as much as possible, but I could still see them. The blood in the cannula coming out of her body was deoxygenated and dark. It went into the ECMO machine that was acting as her heart lungs and kidney. The blood circulated through the machine, was oxygenated, and cleaned. The blood in the cannula that went back into her body was the beautiful red colour associated with health.

Avelynn's body swelled up with oedema and her head swelled to an alarming size. That was difficult to watch. Oedema is the excessive accumulation of serous fluid in the intracellular spaces of tissue. In other words, Avelynn's head, face, and body were abnormally swollen. Normally there's no flesh between the skin and the skull, it's hard to the touch. With Avelynn on ECMO I could press her head like I was pressing down on my thigh, about one centimetre. It was hideous; her eyelids were so swollen that she resembled a puffer fish. It's awful to say, but she looked extremely bloated. My brain tried hard to assimilate the way she looked. This had become the new normal for Avelynn.

I went to bed around eleven, after expressing my breast milk. There was a private cubicle that was nice enough and I listened to music on the radio, trying to relax. It was important that I expressed as much milk as I could. It seemed to be the only positive action that I could take to help support her. That would

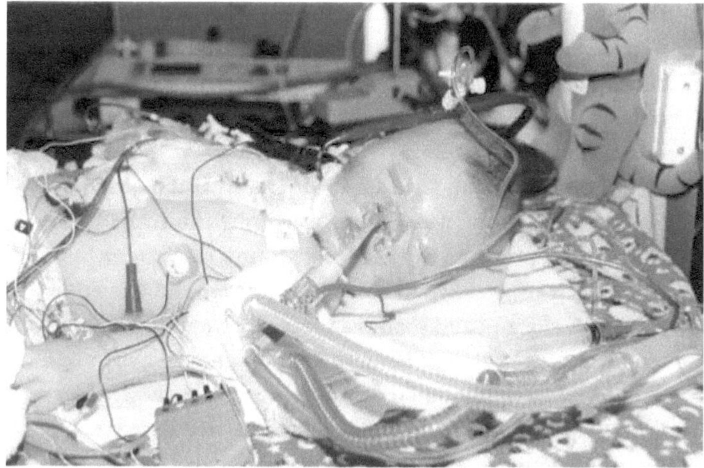

Avelynn still on ECMO

have to suffice for now. But though the lyrics comforted me, I couldn't help but think of Avelynn attached to that machine. With no way to predict what the future held for us, it certainly wasn't a time to feel sorry for myself.

I went back to her and said good night, kissing my finger tips and touching them to her forehead, trying hard not to disturb her. Her eyes looked red and inflamed and had gooey material coming out of them. When I questioned the nurse, she said Avelynn had developed conjunctivitis and had eye ointment in them. How ironic! It was such a normal infection that babies and children got, and I nearly laughed at the simplicity of it.

I kept my ritual of buying myself a chocolate jam donut, convinced that this would keep her heart beating. It was amazing that it didn't keep me awake; I was so emotionally drained that nothing stopped me. I quickly fell into a dead sleep.

> **A bit swollen so I have to have haemofiltration as well to get rid of some fluid.**
>
> **Avelynn's diary, Sunday, 21 November 1999**

> **Expressed around seven this morning, and saw my beautiful little baby, Avelynn. I couldn't help but notice the gorgeous photo of her at around seven weeks old we placed on her bed. I love looking at her in it and I want her back just like**

that—with her heart fixed of course—I noticed the nurses had finally taken off the bandage that usually covers her chest. For the first time I can see the huge cut from the top of her chest—just below her throat—to just past the bottom of her rib cage. It's a beauty—one hell of a scar that anyone would be very proud of. It's healed up well and looks good. So of course I took a photo of Avelynn without the bandage on. Her pressures are hovering around thirteen or fourteen which seems like a miracle to me. Peter and I caught a tram into the city and shared a pizza. We bought Avelynn a wonderful Br'er Rabbit book as we thought the nurses had enough of us reading aloud from *Politically Incorrect Fairy Tales.* The ICU staff has decided Avelynn can have fve millilitres per hour of expressed breast milk. Great stuff! "

My diary, Sunday, 21 November 1999

Sunday, I rose early, expressed my breast milk. Considering how stressed I was, it is hard to believe that I was producing 600-to-800 millilitres daily. I went down to see my beautiful baby, very happy to notice they had removed the dressing from her chest. For the first time, I could see her scar. It's was huge, one I would be very proud to own.

I hoped Avelynn would grow to appreciate her scar and what it means to be a "zipper kid." It's what the members of Heart Kids affectionately call children who have had heart surgery. It's not so much the scar, but what it represents. The scars mean different things to different families. For us, her scar stands for Avelynn's sheer persistence to live, it stands for life. Why not? She fought hard for it. When I saw Avelynn's scar, I was so proud of her. Of course, I took a photo of Avelynn without her bandage.

In the ICU it's common to frequently test the children's blood, and Avelynn was no exception. Her white blood cell count was elevated, indicating a possible infection. This was serious, potentially life threatening. There was no option except to try and fight it with powerful antibiotics.

I was worried about her infection, but of more concern to me, she was incredibly swollen. We were told that sometimes babies on ECMO go into acute renal failure—kidney failure—and the mortality rate is high. To combat this, the nurse explained, she had added haemofiltration to the ECMO machine, which would filter her blood to help remove of waste products. I have since read (www.ncbi.nlm.nih.gov) that acute renal failure, often a part of multiple organ failure, causes generalized oedema and fluid overload, which Avelynn was experiencing.

If Avelynn was to survive she was going to have to fight every single second. Not only were her heart and lungs failing, but now her kidneys. Her strength was incredible, and her will to live unstoppable. She showed an amazing capacity to keep going despite the odds stacked against her. Peter and I stayed by her side with the medical team, willing her to keep fighting.

To help eliminate the waste from her body, she went onto peritoneal dialysis, a treatment for patients with severe chronic kidney disease. The treatment uses the patient's peritoneum—the membrane that lines the abdomen—as a membrane across which fluids and dissolved substances are eliminated from the blood. Her abdomen was flooded with a saline solution which remained for a couple of hours. Waste material—the body's toxins—dissolved in the saline, which was flushed out through a drain tube. I could only imagine how excruciating painful it would be for Avelynn, and I was glad she was on heavy pain killers. It is astonishing to me what the human body can endure. It was only a temporary measure, as we waited and watched to see if she survived.

Peter and I thought if worse came worst, either of us could live quite well with one kidney. Peter said, "Well she can always have one of my kidneys I don't need them both." I said "No way! She can have one of mine." We were arguing about whose kidney she would get, and discussing it in normal tones, as though asking "How many sugars do you want in your coffee?" "Who's picking the kids up tonight, is it me or you?" "What flavour ice cream do you like?"

After only six days we had learnt so much, and been through so much, with Avelynn. We didn't respond as typical parents would have if they had just learned out that their child needed a kidney transplant. We honestly didn't think it was a big deal at the time. If it would have saved her, either of us would gladly have given a kidney; we were arguing about whose kidney it would be. Her doctors never suggested a kidney transplant, we were just talking about it between ourselves.

Chapter 19

In the ICU / ECMO

Avelynn's been on ECMO since Friday and her PA pressures have gone down. We're hopeful, but they keep telling us she's not doing much herself; the machine is doing the work.

Ayla and Kara arrived back today with mum, Sharon, and Rory, her four-month-old.

Peter and I read to Avelynn a lot, especially from the book *When We Were Very Young.* The nurses are probably sick of it, but we're not.

The staff told they will start weaning Avelynn tomorrow and to see how she does—our horrible waiting continues.

My diary, Monday, 22 November 1999

As usual I got up before Peter and headed to the ICU to say a quick hello to my beautiful (though still puffy) baby and check on the night events. When I arrived, they were taking an x-ray. "Why are you taking an x-ray of her head?" I asked the nurse, quite concerned something horrendous had happened overnight. "It's OK, mum," the nurse said, again using their affectionate name all ICU mothers, "Avelynn has a routine x-ray of her brain every day to see if she has behaved herself." They were checking to see if she had a stroke, either a bleed in the brain or a blood clot.

That day, I really didn't want to know, so didn't ask any more questions. I couldn't absorb any more information, having had enough bad news to last a life time. If there was something amiss, they would tell me. It was also routine for Avelynn to have chest x-rays to check if her partly collapsed lungs were inflated or filled with fluid, so they could adjust the machine and continue doing suction on her. Avelynn's lungs were still partly collapsed and filled with fluid, and once again the medical staff was watching and waiting. Peter and I had no choice but to watch and wait alongside them. Waiting was hell and played on our nerves like nothing else.

Avelynn's kidneys were still not working and she was still on peritoneal dialysis, which was horrible to watch. My mind started to drift, and I contemplated her having to go through a kidney transplant. I tried to adjust my thinking and snap myself back to reality and away from those dark thoughts. I didn't ask many questions. After having been through the ringer, for once I wanted only to be close to Avelynn, to read her funny fairy tale books, and to keep up my hopes that she would get better.

Of course there's nothing like bright, energetic, happy children to make you smile, as I did when mum brought Ayla and Kara to the hospital that Sunday. My sister, Sharon, and her baby, Rory, decided to come as well to keep us company. Mum asked me, "How's Avelynn going, Michelle?" I answered, "Hanging in there," but I couldn't talk much in front of Ayla and Kara.

Ayla and Kara came into the ICU with me to see their little sister, but they did not understand. They were unhappy to see Avelynn with the tubes in her, the nurses fussing over her, and all the machines making weird noises. The ICU is not a place for healthy children, and there wasn't much for them to do except sit with me.

One ingenious nurse felt sorry for Ayla. She scrounged some paper and paint, and let Ayla sit and paint by the water basin, out of the way. Ayla thought that was great, and it is still one of her fondest memories of the ICU. Kara didn't want to paint, so she'd complain and fidget on my lap, or mercifully fall asleep on one of the spare couches. We referred to Kara as having "ICU-itis" when the ICU wore Kara out and she fell asleep.

It was tough on the kids when mum, or Sharon, or my sister-in-law weren't around. All Peter and I could do was be with Avelynn, supporting each other. Two and five-year-olds won't stand that lack of attention or be quiet for very long, so Peter or I would take them outside and ensure they had a run-around to get them out of the hospital environment before they went crazy from cabin fever. The weather was lovely, not too hot or too cold, so we could get them out of the stifling atmosphere at the hospital. Sometimes they would go to the Ronald McDonald play ground. Have you ever tried to fit in one of those children's slides? "Come on, mummy, come down the slide," the girls would yell at me. When I had managed to squeeze down one, they'd say, "Do it again!"

So I gave it my best, especially after I looked at their little faces while they tried to convince me it was a good idea. The other kids stayed around for their own amusement in case I got stuck. I was thinking, "Uh, uh! My butt ain't gonna fit in there!" But I managed to squeeze it in and away I went, remembering to duck at the last minute so I didn't crack my head. I saw a couple of other parents have a go, and it was good fun.

Another fun place to go to was the hospital's Starlight Room. This was a great place, with a fun, relaxing atmosphere where we could try to forget about the unpleasantness of life for a while and concentrate on playing with Ayla and Kara. Sometimes, we successfully pretended we were happy making art and crafts with the girls, just like I did at home.

The Starlight Captains were great, they could tell by the looks on our faces that we were experiencing a hard time, and went out of their ways to make the girls giggle and carry on like idiots. The Captains are fantastic people, more like clowns. They help out in the Starlight Room, and since those early days in the hospital, my family has had a lot to do with Starlight Foundation. They granted Avelynn's wish in 2006, and put a playground in our backyard. They are fantastic, and we don't know what we would have done without them. They helped reduce our stress, made the girls laugh, and were the biggest dags out—affectionate Australian slang for complete idiots.

That day, Peter and I took it in turns to look after Ayla and Kara, although both of us were torn whenever we left Avelynn's side. Our biggest fear was not being there if she passed away.

The chances of her coming off ECMO were getting slimmer and slimmer, especially when her kidneys failed. She was still extremely swollen.

> **I still require sedation prior to suction because the nurses don't want to upset my pressures. ECMO, nitric, and drug support have been my life lines.**
>
> **Avelynn's diary, Monday, 22 November 1999**

Chapter 20

Heart Surgery—Again!

Gemma arrived around ten this morning and the girls and I went with her to the fantastic Starlight Room, where the girls made photo frames. Gemma took the girls to her house to give me and Peter a break. Avelynn has been slowly and slightly weaned from ECMO and her pressures have sharply risen again. Her doctors have tried everything, but the bloody stupid PA keep going up. It's hard to take, watching her being connected to the ECMO machine and being controlled by the PA pressure. It's not fair. There's a gorgeous baby in there waiting to come out, but she can't because her PAs are too high. If she comes off ECMO, she'll have a heart attack

All the staff are worried about her—they're reading about other cases, about whatever they can find to save her.

Her surgeon, Dr. Christian Brizard, talked to us and said she's got a very slim chance of coming off the machine and living with a high PA pressure. He wants to do another open-heart surgery to reduce the pressure by implanting a smaller conduit and to put a small hole in her VSD patch. We agreed. It's her last chance and we want our baby back.

Avelynn opened her eyes a little before surgery and was trying very hard to focus on me. I think she knew I was there and was responding to me. If she doesn't make it, at least she saw me before she died and knew that I didn't desert her.

Mum arrived really late with Kim and Marcus, Kim's husband, but I went to bed. I was stuffed but tried to send Avelynn good vibes to keep her going. I still haven't given up hope but it's so hard. Her surgery finished around half-past two Wednesday morning, and I was so thrilled my baby had made it through yet another hurdle. What a fighter she is!.

My diary, Tuesday, 23 November 1999

On Avelynn's the fourth day on ECMO, we faced a huge dilemma. We were asked to make a decision that could save her, if we were right, or could kill her, if we were wrong. A decision that no parent would ever want to face.

We were greatly relieved when Avelynn survived starting on ECMO. The next day was a shock to our systems, but once we then got over our initial shock (though we never really got used to her being on ECMO) we thought everything would be better. We didn't know that, within a few days, Avelynn would, once again, be fighting for her life. Although the ECMO gave her heart and lungs a chance to rest the, her pulmonary hypertension didn't. It remained, as persistent and aggressive as ever, not showing the slightest sign of lessening.

The perfusionist, who operated the ECMO machine, told us that the ventilator settings could be adjusted with the aim of resting her lungs, allowing time for them to recover during the ECMO support. As the lungs recovered, the machine could be weaned and removed. But it wasn't to be in Avelynn's case. They tried to slowly wean Ave off ECMO but were dismayed that her lungs weren't cooperating. Her PA pressures were still as aggressive as ever. They had kept her on ECMO for as long as they thought possible. Unfortunately another obstacle arose, a big one: infection.

Avelynn's white blood cell count spiked and the doctors told us, "We're sorry, but it's impossible to fight an infection whilst on ECMO. She's got so much fluid retention that an infection could wipe her out." She had survived so much; how could it be possible for her to now get a potentially fatal infection? She had been through so much whilst on ECMO, including several bleeds or haemorrhages due to the blood thinners.

The machine itself had a couple of blockages (blood clots) which had to be cleared, threatening her life. Avelynn had haemorrhaged so much, the hospital had run out of A-negative blood, a relatively rare type, and sent for more from another hospital. Until it arrived, they had to give her A-positive, and that caused problems. They told us, "Avelynn has had a major bleed. We had to give her type A-positive blood. Because we can't give her an injection, if she ever gets pregnant, her baby might need a blood transfusion in the womb." Wow! Just when I thought all the fun was over, there was more. What else could go wrong?

Because of the risk of a potentially fatal infection, and because of the risk to her organs, we were told, Avelynn had to come off ECMO to save her life. "Why did it have to happen to Avelynn?" I thought, "Why are so many things going wrong?" I recently watched a couple of medical emergency shows where people were on heart-lung bypass machines and eventually ended up on ECMO. I saw end result of what can sometimes happen with people on ECMO; it's not nice. Like Avelynn, these people on TV swelled up and their organs failed one by one. Eventually they died. I still marvel at how unbelievably strong Avelynn was in the ICU, and how she would not have made it without the dedicated medical team.

When Avelynn was on ECMO, I knew her organs were failing, slowly but surely. When I saw that on TV, it was hard to take; I knew what was happening. I knew that organs start to fail, and she needed to get off ECMO. This was the last, *last* chance at saving her. We simply had no choice.

The decision we faced was:

A. Take her off ECMO and hope that her PA pressures came down (though we all knew her pressure spiked when she was temporarily weaned from ECMO); or

B. Risk another surgery to do something the surgeon had never done before; put a small hole through the patch they had placed over the hole in her heart during her first operation. The doctor hoped the small hole would act as a pressure relief valve and lower her pulmonary hypertension.

It was a huge gamble. The surgeons had never done a procedure like this before. The operation was risky, even when performed by skilled and experienced surgeons. Avelynn, considerably weakened by the ordeal since her first open-heart surgery, would have to survive a second open-heart surgery. There was only a slim chance that she would survive.

We eventually understood that Avelynn might not survive pulmonary hypertension. She needed a new set of lungs. Her heart had been beautifully repaired, but even with the ECMO giving her lungs a chance to rest, the pulmonary hypertension would not abate. We finally realised the pressure in her pulmonary arteries was so extreme, so much higher than normal, it would cause her to have pulmonary crisis, and potentially, a fatal heart attack.

After speaking with a couple of doctors, I left the ICU for a breather. Another doctor saw me looking miserable and we started chatting. That doctor explained to me that fifty percent of the children with cystic fibrosis who needed a new set of lungs didn't make it. That didn't impress me (fifty percent chance of survival sounded pretty high by then) but it really let me know the situation we were in. Peter and I would have handed over everything we owned to save Avelynn; material possessions, our car, they had no value to us, only the life of our daughter.

Avelynn was considerably weakened by a week spent fighting for her life; she'd had several cardiac arrests, her had been transfused with more than three times the volume of her original blood supply, she was on massive pain killers, and her PA pressure was extremely high. There was a considerable risk that the surgery or the anaesthesia would kill her.

We hoped for an option "C" but there wasn't one. We made a decision based on what our hearts told us to do; a decision we knew we had to live with for the rest of our lives if we mucked it up; a decision that had the potential to rip apart our family and our marriage from the strain of losing her. If we were wrong, then we were horribly wrong.

After a long discussion between Peter, myself, and the surgeons, we opted for her to undergo another open-heart surgery, hoping that her wonderful surgeon could perform a miracle and she would survive. That somehow, she had enough fuel left in her tank to fight once again for her right to be here. Just how many lives does a child get? Cats have nine, but Avelynn was way passed that.

Peter had phoned my mum, who came over and sat up with him. But I was past it: burnt out, couldn't cope, couldn't think, couldn't live without my baby. I wanted to crawl into a hole and never return. I didn't want to die, but I felt helpless, like I had fought tooth and nail, and had came up short. I was thinking, "This is it. All the other times have been warm ups. This time, she really does get to visit heaven." For the last couple of days, I had been singing to myself, "Knock, Knock, Knockin on Heaven's Door." When I told one of the nurses, she looked at me as if to ask, "Shall I call the men in white coats for you?" But, hey, that's what was in my head.

I remember saying good-bye to Avelynn as, once again, we signed papers. I wished beyond anything else in my life that she would somehow be able to hang in there and come out the other side. I couldn't cope, I had been through the wringer, and I needed to cuddle myself in bed and sleep. That was the first and only time, of all the times we've been to hospital, that I thought I would to snap and break down. I didn't even talk to my mum, who had driven from two hours away.

"Michelle, wake up! Michelle, wake up!" "What? What? What's happened? Is she okay?" I asked Peter as he tried to wake me. "Yes, she made it!" Peter replied. I promptly fell back into an exhausted sleep.

Chapter 21

ICU—Up From the Grave

Things still steady. Avelynn's is now critical, but not extremely critical. We learnt there is a difference between "extremely critical"(could pass away any second), "very critical" (quite unstable and could pass if thing get worse), and just "critical" (not out of the woods, but not about to pass away). Sure, her condition could quickly change, and I am not sure how the doctors analyse the situation, but that was how Peter and I understood it, and it helped us understand the risks.

Mum left at eleven this morning, looking as stuffed as I felt. Sharon came at four and left at eight this evening. She was a great help to us and the kids.

My diary, Wednesday, 24 November 1999

The morning after was like magic, I think the magic faerie had arrived in the night. Not only had Avelynn pulled through the operation okay, she was doing well, and they had taken out her PA line. We noticed that immediately, asking, "Hey! Where's her PA line? God, don't you need it? What if her pressures are still high?" "Well, we won't know, and at this point it doesn't matter." He explained that, because she had a hole in her heart acting as a pressure relief valve, then they didn't need to know what her pressures were doing.

But I did, I wanted to know, and was quite stressed-out not knowing. During the previous eight days, Peter and I had become accustomed to watching her monitor, rather than watching Avelynn. We had become rather attached to watching what her PA's were doing; it helped us to control our fear and to prepare ourselves for another episode. Now, watching the monitor was a waste of time; it didn't show her PAs, so we were left without the security of knowing what they were. I didn't find it reassuring, but I understood the logic. Why worry about her PA pressure when it was now irrelevant?

Wow! I could hardly believe Avelynn was off ECMO. She had somehow survived the operation and seemed to be coping. She's so strong! Peter and I can only be strong for her, hopeful that she will eventually come home with us. We were not yet out of the woods, not by a long shot. Avelynn was still bloated; still had the peritoneal dialysis attached, working as her kidneys; still had partially collapsed, fluid-filled lungs. We were still playing the waiting game, but her chances had improved considerably.

For the eight days when Avelynn had been fighting for her life, we felt that we couldn't leave the hospital and certainly couldn't relax. Today, we finally felt we could go out. Avelynn seemed a lot more stable with the a life-saving pressure relief valve, the hole in her patch across the VSD. Our anxiety eased somewhat, knowing that she was no longer at risk for a heart attack.

We thought an outing into town with Ayla and Kara would lift all of our spirits. It was one month and one day until Christmas, and Melbourne was celebrating in style. We saw the famous and enchanting Christmas windows at the Myer department store. They are amazing. I had never seen them before, so I was as excited as the girls. We didn't stay away from the hospital and Avelynn for very long but the outing did us a world of good.

Today seemed especially hard for Peter and me. We had been struggling with Avelynn's unpredictable condition for eight days, the longest days of my life. Now that she was off ECMO and seemed to be holding steady, we finally let some of our emotions out. Both of us were all over the place, and I alternated between being upset and being angry at life.

On one hand, I was hopeful everything would turn out okay. I was happier than the day before, but I couldn't let myself get excited. We didn't know how she's would to be the next day, when we could leave, or what we should be doing. There was still a huge question mark hanging over us. I wanted a time-frame, but the hospital staff did not have one to give us. We had so many questions and so few answers. "Will we be home for Christmas?" "Will Avelynn's kidneys start working again?" "When will she be weaned off the ventilator?" If we were there for much longer I was going to have to buy summer clothes, the weather was warming.

> **Back to ICU without ECMO following another repair to my heart and requiring different form of drugs to control my pulmonary hypertension.**
>
> **Avelynn's diary, Wednesday, 24 November 1999**

> **Expressed and saw my beautiful baby this morning on my own before I had breakfast. She's been allowed to slowly wake up from her heavy sedation and is trying to open her eyes with a lot of effort and wriggled ever so slightly. Today is the first time I have seen her do that in the ICU since her first heart surgery.**
>
> **I felt like crying seeing her like that, so helpless. I love her so much, and she's too cute and adorable to be going through this. But she is a fighter, so we have to draw our strength from her, and be strong in order to give her hope and encouragement.**
>
> **She's stable, which is fantastic, but her pressures are too high. I can envision being here for Christmas, although I hope not.**
>
> **We all walked up to the shops and had Chinese take-away.**
>
> **My diary, Thursday, 25 November 1999**

Today I felt better, and even let myself envision taking Avelynn home. I had been scared to do that before, in case I jinxed her chances. Now, it almost seemed real, she might be getting better. She was not as bloated and no longer required peritoneal dialysis. Her kidneys had decided to start working again, thank goodness, one less thing to worry about.

Her lungs were still full of fluid and still partially collapsed. X-rays of her head did not show any blood clots or bleeds. What a relief, no more heart attacks, and no more fighting for her life. She was finally coming up from the grave, and we again began to hope in our future together as a family.

During the first eight days in the ICU, we were so focused on Avelynn's survival that we hardly communicated with other parents. We passed a lot of people like ships in the night, not talking to them. Although our pain was great, we couldn't voice our fears. Passing others in the parents' accommodation, I could tell by looking at their faces that they were having really hard times coping with their child's illness. Their body language was like mine, loudly saying, "I can't talk now." We all internalised our thoughts and couldn't communicate.

Peter and I didn't even want to talk to each other. This is the first time in twelve years that I have spoken about my feelings, at the time it was just too difficult. In the ICU, I shut down; I became a zombie. After the first forty-eight hours, I didn't even cry. All I did was ensure my baby was okay and remained strong for her. It wouldn't have done anyone any good for me to crack up, especially as I had to look after Ayla and Kara. They needed me more than ever; Avelynn was their baby as well. At two and five, they were too young to understand, and had no experience with anything like this. I couldn't expect them to cope, so we had to cope for them.

The most wonderful occurrences that I witnessed in the ICU were the acceptance parents had towards their children, no matter what illness or disability they had. After Avelynn came off ECMO, and I was ready to engage in conversation again, I struck up a conversation with a parent next to me. He told me how his five-week-old baby girl had been securely strapped into her baby capsule. Another car had hit his from the side, causing it to roll. The impact had thrown his little girl around in her capsule.

His daughter survived, but looked as if a watermelon were attached to the side of her head. She kept having seizures and the news wasn't good; she appeared to have severe brain damage. The amazing thing was when her dad told me, "Oh, it doesn't matter, you know. I can't read or write, so what does it matter if my kid can't?"

To me, that was total acceptance of his child; he would love her no matter what. By the love in his eyes when he looked at his child, I knew that she would be well cared for and nurtured. He was standing vigil over her, just as Peter and I were with Avelynn.

We met many wonderful parents in the hospital, both in the ICU and in the parents' accommodation. Many of them were really strong, and only a few appeared not to be coping well. There were families from all over Australia and from overseas as well. Those who were lucky enough to be there received first-class medical attention. Some could afford to come; others were sponsored by one of the tremendous Australian charities, which cover the entire cost of the child's surgery.

It was wonderful for us to see and speak to parents who had, like us, been through hell and back. We offered each other wonderful companionship, support, and understanding. It was always a challenge, after we got to know parents really well in the ICU, when their child passed away after appearing to fight just as hard as Avelynn. That was tough. We never knew what had happened and we couldn't comfort the parents.

The ICU is a tough place for parents. You were constantly forced to steel yourself against what was happening all around. Avelynn was in the middle of three beds along one side of the room, and there were three more beds along the opposite wall. We learnt to develop tunnel vision, like a race horse wearing blinkers. The horse is not distracted by what's going on around him because the blinkers force the horse to look ahead. We quickly learnt to look straight ahead and not at what was going on around us.

We didn't have this problem for the first eight days when Avelynn was fighting for her life, and we could only concentrate on her. Once she came off ECMO, I started to notice more, and had to apply my blinkers. I really didn't want to know what was going on around me, although I did get to know a few parents who wanted to talk or who we met at the morning teas.

> **I had another head scan, so far so good. Mum and dad must be so relieved. I better behave myself.**
>
> **Avelynn's diary, Thursday, 25 November 1999**

> **Ayla came with me to express this morning. Avelynn's PA pressures went too high last night and the nurse gave her another injection of muscle relaxant. When I came in she was only starting to open her eyes up again. Avelynn responded well to our voices and wiggled a little. She looks so cute!**
>
> **Mum picked the girls up and is taking them tonight so Peter and I can spend some time with each other, and together in the ICU with Avelynn. Ayla's okay with the plans to go to grandma's. Kara's really needs my one-to-one attention which I can't give her much of, so she's is misbehaving at every opportunity. Kara did not want to go to grandma's. I feel sorry for her and wish I could spend more time with her, but I am emotionally strained and need the break.**
>
> **Avelynn's been stable all day which is such a relief. The doctors have decided she can be weaned off morphine, some of the heart drugs, and the ventilator. Oh, wow! I feel like today is a miracle; it appears Avelynn has finally turned the corner.**
>
> **My diary, Friday, 26 November 1999**

Arriving, with Ayla, to see Avelynn this morning, I was alarmed to earn that her pressures had sky-rocketed last night, and she had to be sedated again. I was very pleased that she was trying to open her eyes and focus on me and Ayla when she heard our voices. Maybe she really had been listening when we read to her for hours, as she had no trouble recognising our voices. Ayla's much happier to come with me to the ICU now that Avelynn is off ECMO. She had found it hard to cope with seeing her baby sister on such a huge machine.

Avelynn even wiggled a little bit so, wow, that was fantastic to see! We had become so accustomed to her not being allowed to move a muscle that to see her wiggling seemed like a major event and made me extremely happy.

Mum picked up Ayla and Kara. Ayla was happy to go, but Kara tried to cling to me like a monkey to a tree. My poor baby! She did not understand what was happening, and wanted me, rather than grandma. But I was adamant; I needed a break, and Peter and I wanted to be together with Avelynn in the ICU.

We had been sitting with Avelynn for most of the day. The doctor thought we should get out of the hospital for a much-needed break. He knew the girls were with my mum, and eventually said, "Listen, you guys. You need to go out and do something. Go and have a drink, or dinner, or something, for goodness sakes. But don't have too much to drink and do what the other lady did." "What was that?" I asked, my interest piqued, wondering what a stressed out mum might do. The doctor elaborated, "Well, I told these parents to go out and have a drink; there's a nice pub up the road. The mum got drunk, climbed on a table to do the 'Cha-cha,' fell off, and broke her leg." "Oh, wow! No way! That's bad!" I thought, and made a mental note not to drink much. We ended up having dinner at a hotel within walking distance of the hospital, and had a fantastic time. No broken limbs or other excitement.

Peter and I went to the Victorian Market; mostly just browsed. I bought a few summer clothes. The weather has turned much warmer, and I didn't bring enough with me from Perth. At half-past one, we had just finished lunch when mum arrived with the girls. I was a bit pissed-off at her. I had asked her to bring the girls back later on in the afternoon, I had just returned from the market, and I hadn't seen Avelynn, except much earlier that morning.

Apparently my sister, Kimberley, had to go food shopping and she was driving in order to give mum a rest, and she wanted to drop the girls off earlier. What a bummer! I was glad to see my beautiful girls, but it meant that Peter and I had to take it in turns to see Avelynn, and alternate playing

> **and taking care of the girls. We did not get any rest and the girls were hard work.**
>
> **Some friends came in today, our only visitors outside my immediate family since Avelynn's first surgery. It was great to have visitors and to catch up with some good friends.**
>
> **Avelynn is much the same as yesterday, but she slept more.**
>
> **My diary, Saturday, 27 November 1999**

Peter and I had waited for the girls to go with mum before we ventured out to the Victorian Market. We had caught a tram and wondered around the huge market where, it seemed, you could buy practically anything. I was only looking for some lighter summer clothes to fit me. Stupidly, I thought we would only be here for ten days and had only brought winter clothes. By that Saturday, the weather had warmed up beautifully. I was rapidly shrinking back to my pre-pregnant weight, as I tended. I knew most of my friends envied my ability to do this, but I desperately needed something to wear other than pregnancy clothes. I was rather pleased to have found a few items.

Around half-past one, Peter and I were enjoying lunch when mum walked in with Kimberley, Ayla, and Kara. We had thought we had plenty of time before they were due, and had planned to sit together with Avelynn. It was sheer luxury that we hadn't had to arrange lunch for the girls, and we had been trying to relax over a nice meal before we went to see Avelynn.

This was the reason that I had asked mum not to come before three. They didn't even have the courtesy to phone us up and tell us they were coming early. Of course I wanted the girls back with me, but they were a handful. Their early return meant that either Peter or I couldn't see Avelynn; one of us would have to stay with Ayla and Kara. Kara would flatly refuse to see Avelynn, crying and complaining if we forced her. Coping with Kara and her stress had become a strain.

Ayla was older and better able to cope, but naturally preferred to be out playing at the Ronald McDonald playground or in the hospital's Starlight Room with the "funny Captains." The girls wanted their baby back; they didn't want to see her attached to funny tubes or listen to the machines go "ping" or "pong," or make all sorts of other weird sounds.

Avelynn was much the same today but sleepier. Her lungs are still partially collapsed with lots of fluid in them. The doctors seemed pleased with her progress; she was headed in the right direction. Peter and I were relieved, but still stressed; that's why we snapped at mum and Kimberley. They had been fantastic supports for us and given us a lot of time that we could spend together with Avelynn.

Ayla and Kara were happy to be with us. They asked to stay with us at the hospital, and not go to grandma's again. I tried to convince them otherwise, but I knew their stress levels were at an all-time high, They needed me now as much as Avelynn did.

Peter and I worked out a bit of a time table around the older girls, and Avelynn, and my expressing milk every couple of hours. It was all we could do to keep a balance and maintain some normalcy for the Ayla and Kara. They had given up asking when would be going home, and seemed happy instead going to the Starlight Room, or to the outside park, or to Ronald McDonald's playground. Those had become their new norm.

At half past six, I went down and said a big hello to my beautiful baby girl. I'd slept well but would probably have stayed in bed all day if I had that luxury.

I returned to the ICU just after nine. Avelynn was really upset and crying. Because of the tubes in her throat, it's a silent cry, and surely one of the saddest things I've ever seen. I had tears in my eyes, and I just wanted to pick her up.

She's been coughing up a lot; you can't actually hear it, but the nurses showed me how to tell, and they must suction heaps of mucus. The mucus is from the fluid that is still in her lungs. The top right and bottom left lobes of her lungs are still deflated and filled with mucus.

> **She's stable and about the same as yesterday. The staff are still weaning her off the heart drugs. For the first time in twelve very long days, I cuddled Avelynn. She was on a pillow and went to sleep in my arms—it was great!**
>
> **My diary, Sunday, 28 November 1999**

I had slept well enough the previous night, but still felt really sleepy, probably the effect of all those jam donuts.

Avelynn was really upset that morning. She had slowly been weaned off morphine and could move some. Without all of the drugs, she became more aware of her surroundings, and wanted to be held. I had not yet been allowed to pick her up, but Avelynn's nurse had seen the longing on my face, and asked, "Do you want to have a hold of Avelynn?" "Really? Can I? Will she be okay? Will she be able to cope with being moved?" I replied, not quite believing what the nurse had asked. I waited, with baited breath, for the nurse to ask the doctors if it was okay, rubbing my hands together in anticipation. "Yes! It's fine, you can have a hold," she told me.

Oh, wow! Finally, the moment that I was afraid might never arrive. For eight excruciatingly hard days, while she had fought for her life, I had not dared to allow myself to even think of holding Avelynn in my arms. Now it seemed a miracle was about to happen, and I was a part of it. The longing and the painful wait were finally over. "Okay, sit this chair and put this pillow across your legs," the nurse told me. Sitting down was still very painful for me; my broken coccyx was incredible sore. But I hardly felt the pain as I sat as instructed with a pillow across my legs. The nurse had to undo wires, change around leads, rearrange the oxygen, and move the oxygen-saturation sensor from her hand to her big toe, but, finally, she placed Avelynn on the pillow, her head resting on my right arm. Avelynn cuddled close to me, looked at me through sleepy eyes, and promptly feel asleep.

I had tears in my eyes, not believing how fortunate I was to hold my precious baby once again. My whole body had ached for this moment. To be able to comfort her, to feel her breathing against me, to pat her hair, and to gently trace the outline of her face with my finger, seemed such a gift. Yet, it was a gift many parents take for granted, as I had before Avelynn's predicament. It was pure bliss, even with my extremely sore backside, which reminded me that I should not have been sitting. Ignoring that discomfort, I was extremely happy, had felt like the happiest mum alive. Peter looked on, a wee bit envious, but understood that today, I needed to hold her more than he did. Ayla and Kara patted her head, looking bewildered, not understanding why Avelynn was now allowed to have a cuddle, but pleased all the same. The nurse was wonderful. She let me hold Avelynn for an hour and it felt so good. I could almost believe we would take her home with us.

Avelynn's lungs delayed the proceedings. They were still partially collapsed and filled with fluid. Her strong heart was coping amazingly well, considering the beating it had taken. Many times, I had heard the nurses and doctors mention that Avelynn's heart was one of the strongest they had come across; they still couldn't understand how she had survived. With no prior experience I too was amazed, but not as much as the medical team.

During the hour I had held Avelynn, I had hope in my little baby. Looks can be so deceiving, Avelynn was so much stronger than she seemed. The doctors had mentioned several times that they'd hardly ever seen such a tough child, such incredible persistence to live. Peter and I often joked about from whom she got her persistence and stubbornness; I am pretty sure it came from us both.

Avelynn was being slowly weaned off her massive drug support. If she continued to improve, we should soon be out of the ICU. The doctors were also optimistic, although they were somewhat cautious, and would not set a date.

Avelynn still required frequent suctioning to clear the secretions coming from her lungs. She was more awake, and tried to cough on her own, but she was still attached to the ventilator by a breathing tube in her trachea.

> **Wow, now my ventilation is less. I have now progressed to CPAP, so I am doing all the breathing. The nitric is lower too. My new doctor wanted to get rid of the breathing tube but I said, "No! Wait because of my spit—too much." Mum had a cuddle. My sisters wanted to cuddle me, too, but will have to wait.**
>
> **Avelynn's diary, Sunday, 28 November 1999**

> **They've weaned Avelynn off morphine and they moved the endotracheal tube to the back of her throat. So now Avelynn can cough up the mucus, and try to help herself and clear her lungs. She's been very sleepy, but wakes up now and again, and looks at us as if she's checking up.**
>
> **Avelynn's finally is weaned off the nitric oxide gas that's been mixed in with her oxygen and her pressures have stayed the same. YEAH!**
>
> **Avelynn is now onto CPAP (it's a constant pressure of oxygen) and they put the tube further up so it now sits just above her throat. I can hear her little tiny cry like it's far away, and it's very rough because the tubes had been down her throat for two weeks. My poor baby! My heart goes out to her.**
>
> **My diary, Monday, 29 November 1999**

I'm thrilled that Avelynn is finally off morphine; I can only hope she isn't having withdrawals. No, I am just kidding. That's one of the reasons the doctors slowly weaned her off it—to avoid any painful withdrawals—as she had been on the drug for two weeks. Morphine is a fantastic drug that can be used for long periods of time to treat moderate to severe pain. I felt more optimistic now that Avelynn was off morphine; it proved to me that she was recovering and one step closer to moving out of the ICU. Of course, Avelynn still had pain killers, but they were not as strong.

Today was a day for changes. Avelynn was put onto "Continuous Positive Airway Pressure" (CPAP) which eliminated the need for tracheal intubation. In other words, she no longer had the large tube down her throat; it had been exchanged for a much smaller one through a nostril and into the top part of her throat, where the slight pressure keeps the upper airway open. This change had enabled Avelynn to cough up the mucous from the fluid in her lungs, which is essential if they are going to reinflate properly. Avelynn is now breathing on her own. Wow! It's was so exciting to know that her heart and lungs have recovered enough to take over from the machine.

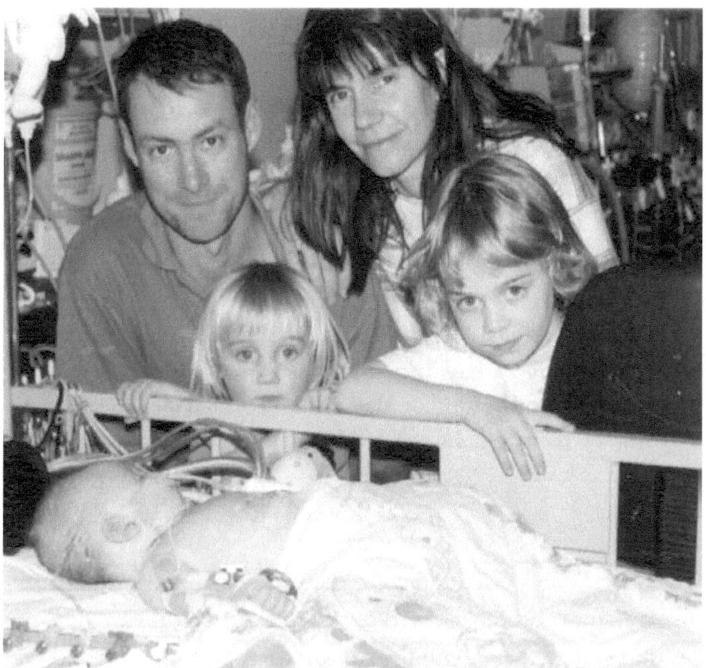

Avelynn on Cpap with Dad, Kara, Mum, and Ayla

Although it was fantastic for Avelynn to be on Cpap, it was sad to hear her pitiful cry, which reminded me of a tiny, week-old kitten I once looked after at the vets. Tears had rolled down her face when she cried; it was hard for me not to rip her off that bloody bed and hold her for dear life. Once again, I had to play the waiting game. At least this time, I was waiting to hold onto her, not see if she survived the night.

I am doing very well, as I have progressed to nasal CPAP. Better behave myself so I can join my sisters, Kara and Ayla and my cat, waiting for me at home.

Avelynn's diary, Monday, 29 November 1999

Weaned off nitric oxide—yeah!—I sure am glad that's gone. As it's the drug that helped to keep the PA vessels open, so I figured Avelynn was well on her way to recovery if they were confident enough to take her off nitric oxide. She's been coughing up a lot of mucus, but that is what she needs to do to help clear her lungs and get out of here.

Had another cuddle with Avelynn, for an hour or so, and it was absolutely fantastic. She fell asleep in my arms again and was very comfortable.

One of the fantastic male nurses took her stitches out, but and had a little trouble. Some of them were embedded in her skin.

Peter, Ayla, and Kara went back to Sharon's house for the night. Though I hated to see them go, and knew I would miss them, it was kind of nice and quiet. I decided to spend most of the night in the ICU, just watching my baby at peace at last.

My diary, Tuesday, 30 November 1999

Oh, wow! When I went down to the ICU, the nurse proudly told me Avelynn had been weaned completely off her nitric oxide, the gas that was mixed in with the oxygen to help keep her blood vessels open. The nitric oxide was critically important. It may have helped ease the pressure slightly when Avelynn's blood pressure was extremely high before her second heart surgery. But now it was gone, and Avelynn was improving every day. I had taken it as a sign that she was closer to leaving ICU. Wow! Imagine if we could be home for Christmas, only twenty-five days away.

I couldn't believe how stupid I was. I had done only minimal Christmas shopping before we left for Melbourne. I was so fixated about being there for only ten days, it never occurred to me that I wouldn't have time for shopping. I was madly trying to calculate the odds and kept asking myself, "Should I go out and start shopping in Melbourne? What if Ayla, who is really cluey, discovers that I have bought presents? Will I have enough time to shop if we get back to Perth in time for Christmas? What if I can't find the presents they really want? If I do shop in Melbourne, how am I going to fit the presents into our suitcase?" On and on my thoughts went. The medical team were fairly tired of me asking "When do you think Avelynn can go home?" I had not dared to ask that question until we got out of the ICU. Then I could start asking the new doctors, up on the cardiac ward, called "7 West."

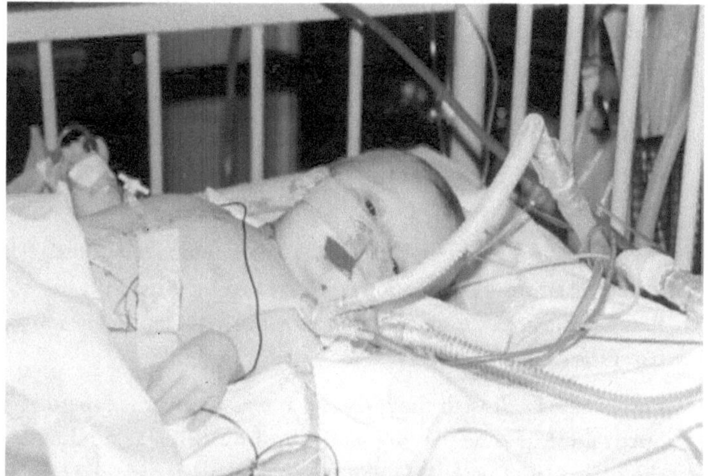

Avelynn, slowly recovering on Cpap

On a positive note, I felt extremely lucky that I could now have these thoughts. It was sheer luxury not to have to think "What if Avelynn does not make it back to Perth?" The fact that I was now contemplating what I could buy her for Christmas seemed amazing; I felt I was the luckiest person alive!

The girls needed a breather, so Peter decided to go to Sharon's when she left. The girls would not leave without one of us firmly attached. Kara was a nightmare; an extremely unhappy two-year-old. Her world had turned upside down, her stress levels were high, and she was not coping. Peter and I tried our best but it was hard on all of us. I was glad I had brought the girls with us to Melbourne—I didn't regret it for a second—but our stay was taking its toll on us all. I did not envy Peter for getting out of the hospital; the only place I wanted to be was at Avelynn's side.

I spent most of the night beside Avelynn, drinking coffee and eating way too much chocolate. And yes, I even ate my chocolate jam donut, thank you very much!

> **Still on nasal CPAP, but one of the fantastic nurses gave me some lovely medicine, and I slept really well. I feel like a new girl lately. Still having lots of secretions which make me a little grumpy at times, my wonderful male nurse looked after me again today. Oh, I had a lovely cuddle from mum and learned to play raspberries (blow bubbles with my spit)**
>
> **Avelynn's diary, Tuesday, 30 November 1999**

> **Avelynn went onto CPAP Monday, and they decided to take it off today. She's only got a small oxygen tube in her nose instead to help her breathe.**
>
> **Avelynn was finally well enough to commence her physiotherapy sessions, which are supposed to help her still-deflated right upper lung. I hope it soon inflates and recovers from the damage it received.**
>
> **Peter came back with the girls and it was great to see them. Spent a lot of time playing games and mucking around at the playground with Ayla and Kara, while Peter looked after Avelynn.**
>
> **My diary, Wednesday, 1 December 1999**

The speed at which Avelynn was improving was absolutely amazing, she is such a trooper! Despite having her right upper lung deflated and filled with mucus, she was going really well. The medical team were still very happy with her and were also amazed at her speedy recovery. I asked the nurses a couple of questions about her lungs. They told me that the right lung has three lobes but the left has only two to provide room for the heart.

I had become quite fascinated about lungs by this stage since they were the cause of most of her massive problems. I wanted to know when Avelynn's lung would start to inflate and if this lung would cause distress in the future. They said they really didn't know but were hopeful she would keep recovering.

Today, the medical team started her physiotherapy treatment to help inflate her right lung, which would help to ease her breathing, and increase her oxygen saturation.

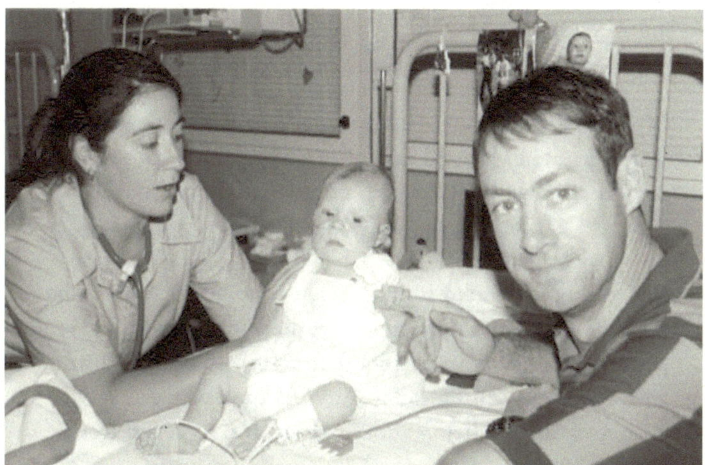

Physio time with Dad

I was pretty scared by Avelynn's physio treatment. The physiotherapist would put her in a blue plastic chair that forced her to sit up, making her really uncomfortable. But it was essential for her to sit up for as long as she could tolerate to help inflate her lung. Then the therapist would fold a towel across Avelynn's back until it was a good thickness and proceed to whack her until she coughed. Avelynn hated this, and would cry her tiny cry. My heart would go out to her; I think I hated it as much as Avelynn, but knew it would make the difference of us getting out of hospital sooner and lessening the risks of infection.

Avelynn had physio three times today. Though I knew it was good for her, I cringed each time I saw the physio approaching her. Her right upper lung had no choice except to inflate or keep being whacked until it did; that was my take on it!

Avelynn also had her CPAP taken out which was very fast, bearing in mind that she only had it put in on Monday, two days before. I was starting to imagine writing on the wall with a big arrow: "Exit the ICU this way," "Leave now if you dare." Something like that.

Things were looking up. I was happy to spend a lot of time with Ayla and Kara, playing "silly buggers," as I affectionately called it; chasing each other around the playground.

> **My wonderful nurse gave me something to sleep overnight, isn't it great? I was still fast asleep when mum came to see me. As usual with all the secretions around my mouth.**
>
> **Avelynn's diary, Wednesday, 1 December 1999**

> **I'm feeling frustrated today. I want to comfort Avelynn by picking her up and putting her on the boob. I am sick of expressing and really want my life to return to normal. I worried about everything today and feel torn between staying with Avelynn and being with my beautiful Ayla and Kara.**
>
> **They were going to send Avelynn up to 7 West today, the cardiac ward, but there's no room so she's in the ICU for another night.**
>
> **I had another cuddle which helped calm me down but I need more than one hour per day and I miss the close contact with her.**
>
> **My diary, Thursday, 2 December 1999**

The incredible excitement that I had felt about finally leaving the ICU either that day or the next, as we had been promised, was almost too much for me to bear. Frustration, coupled with anxiety about leaving the security of the ICU, played on my nerves and left me an emotional mess. Trying not to show how uptight I felt, I had played with Ayla and Kara as usual at the Ronald McDonald playground. I had chased the girls like an idiot, had drunk too much coffee, and had eaten way too much chocolate.

Peter and I were torn between realising how lucky we were to still have had our beautiful daughter with us, knowing she was getting better, and not wanting to leave the security of the ICU. The thought of going up to the cardiac ward, 7 West, was daunting for us. We felt safe in the ICU and had gotten to know the nurses and doctors so well they seemed like friends. I had heard that the anxiety and fear we faced leaving the ICU was quite common. As with all the challenges I have faced, I decided to deal with it head on.

On a positive note, I realised that as soon as Avelynn was transferred, I would be able to pick her up and have a more active role in her care. Trust me, I had every intention of doing that. We could also sleep by her side, which is not allowed in the ICU. I would be able to breast feed again, or attempt to. So there were lots of great things to look forward to.

Apparently there was no room in 7 West; we had raised our hopes for nothing, had to spend another night in the ICU. Hopefully, our last!

> **I had physiotherapy today—I can't believe I've still got a sore bum!**
>
> **Left the ICU this morning around eleven. YEAH!!!!!**
>
> **My diary, Friday, 3 December 1999**

On Friday, 3 December, we finally left the ICU. What a momentous occasion for us. We had come so far, our psychological make-up had changed. We were no longer the same people who entered the hospital only eighteen short days ago. Peter and I had known we were tough, but it seemed we also "bred 'em tough." Avelynn's strength had to have been the most amazing feat I had ever witnessed. I still shake my head in wonder as to how she possibly won the day.

Though we were apprehensive about leaving the ICU, we knew that leaving was a step towards going home. Going back to Perth, to our friends, to our beautiful Burmese pussy cats, to our crazy dog, and to the wonderful Army family that had been closely following our harrowing tale.

As the nurses wheeled Avelynn's bed up the hall towards 7 West, I reflected on the trials and tribulations our family had been through. Some would say we've all been to hell and back, but Avelynn even more so. I could only wonder what the future had in store for my amazing little red head.

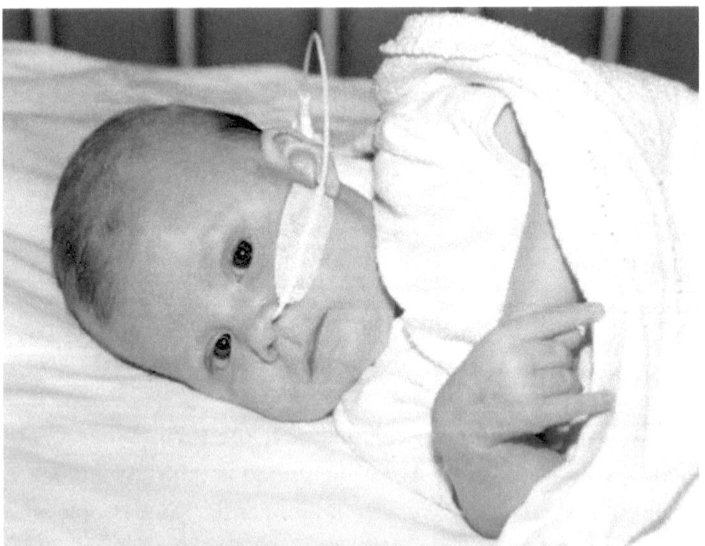

Avelynn, 13 weeks, in Perth

Avelynn celebrating Christmas with Ayla and Kara, 1999

Avelynn with Mum, New Years Eve, 1999

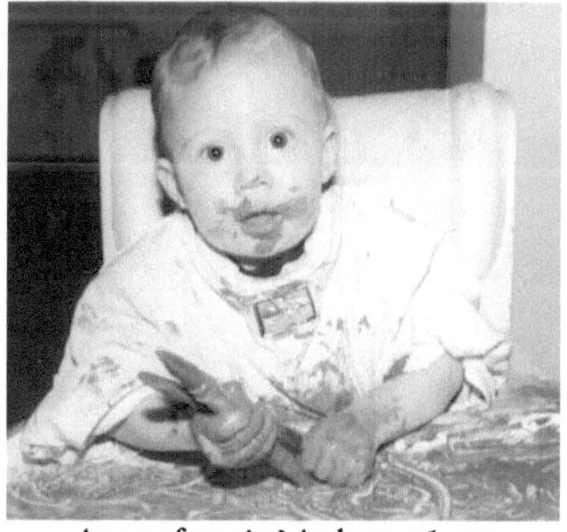

Anyone for paint? Avelynn at 1 year

www.ingramcontent.com/pod-product-compliance
Lightning Source LLC
LaVergne TN
LVHW090936080826
845145LV00003B/770

9780987241528